Education and
the End of Work

EDUCATION AND THE END OF WORK

A new philosophy of work and learning

John White

CASSELL

for Louise

Cassell
Wellington House, 125 Strand, London WC2R 0BB
PO Box 605, Herndon, VA 20172

First published 1997

British Library Cataloguing-in-Publication Data
A catalogue record for this book is available from the British Library.

ISBN 0-304-33947-4 (hardback)
0-304-33948-2 (paperback)

Edited and typeset by Ruth Noble, Peebles, Scotland
Printed and bound in Great Britain by Redwood Books, Trowbridge, Wiltshire

Contents

	ACKNOWLEDGMENTS	vii
ONE	WORK AS WE KNOW IT	1
	Introduction	1
	The meaning of work	3
	The work culture	10
	Education and the work culture	16
TWO	PHILOSOPHERS AT WORK ON WORK	19
	Introduction	19
	Work and human nature	20
	The right to meaningful work	30
	Work and labour	36
	Challenging centrality	40
THREE	WORK AND WELL-BEING	45
	Introduction	45
	Human well-being	45
	Autonomous work	48
	Heteronomous work	53
	Towards the activity society	60
	Distributing work	65
FOUR	EDUCATION AND THE FUTURE OF WORK	69
	Introduction	69
	Scenario 1: Status quo	69
	Scenario 2: Beyond the work society	74
	Education for the activity society	78
	Clarifying educational aims	85
FIVE	EDUCATION AND WORK: VEHICLES OF LEARNING	97
	Work and learning	97
	Parents' responsibilities	101
	Schools and work	104
	Remaking the school day	111
	Post-school learning	118
	Conclusion	120
	BIBLIOGRAPHY	121
	INDEX	124

Acknowledgements

I am grateful for their comments to several audiences to whom I have read papers based on the ideas in this book. These include participants in the Philosophy of Education Research Seminar at the Institute of Education University of London; staff and students at the Catholic University of Leuven, Belgium; and members of the Philosophy of Education Society of Great Britain at the 1996 Annual Conference at New College, Oxford.

I would also like to thank my colleagues, Professor Richard Aldrich, for his reactions to an early draft, and Mike Coles for discussions on vocational education in Britain. Terry McLaughlin was most helpful in keeping me abreast of new reading in the area. I could not begin to spell out how much I owe to my wife, Patricia White for her comments on this work as well as the other productions and co-productions of the last thirty-odd years of our working together.

ONE

Work as we know it

INTRODUCTION

'Why should I let the toad *work*
Squat on my life?
Can't I use my wit as a pitchfork
And drive the brute off?'
from Philip Larkin *Toads*

A clip from *The Independent*: ' "She has never stopped working 19 hours a day," says her friend Lord Archer. "She has nothing else in life. She can't stop, and she doesn't know how to. She starts at 6 am and they have to drag her to bed at night." "Work is a drug for her," said one insider, "and she's a junkie".'[1]

What gives Margaret Thatcher highs is a downer for others – including the Japanese man, reported, also in *The Independent*, as having killed himself after working for seventeen months without a day off.[2]

I have a growing pile of newspaper cuttings like these about work. My daily paper – no guesses which – cannot leave the topic alone. The *'Work can kill' warning* piece just mentioned sits on top of *'We must break our 45-hours-a-week habit'*. 'Work, work, work,' subheadlines Polly Toynbee. 'And this was supposed to be the "quality of life decade".

'You're cabbaged when you get home'. The latest of my clippings, like many of the others, is about the British – 'the workaholics of Europe'. The average UK working week, at 43.1 hours, is the highest in Europe. 'The number of British workers putting in weeks of more than 50 hours has grown by a third'. 'While working hours on the Continent have been retreating, in Britain there has been a steady growth'.[3]

Work patterns in the 1920s were more leisurely – at least for some. The City merchant banker Henry Tiarks, for instance. 'Rising early, he rode every morning and then motored up to the office in the Bentley with his father from the family's country house at Chislehurst, in Kent. Business permitting, he returned home in the late afternoon to play polo and then it was back to town for dinner in Mayfair or Belgravia. Strikingly handsome and immaculately mannered, he was a catch for any hostess's table.'[4]

Attitudes to work differ. For the downsized, it can be a receding memory of financial security and office camaraderie; for the downshifted, the victory of convention over having a life of one's own. Interviewed beneath his apple trees in Hampstead Garden Suburb, Andy Blackford revealed that he once 'earned £80,000 a year, ate at the best restaurants on expenses and had four new Jaguars in the space of five years. And then one day he suddenly thought: "What's the bloody point?"' – and resigned at the age of 46. 'The life we led demanded as much and slightly more than we earned. I had a baby I only saw in the middle of the night, when she was giving me grief. I lived this frantic life of earning and consuming – I had to consume to sustain the earning – but what for? It seemed meaningless.'[5]

My own type of work, philosophising, sometimes proves a useful practical resource. Not only to throw light on the meaningfulness or otherwise of Andy Blackford's life, but also to bring order to our decade's bewilderments about whether work is to be loved or hated – about its place in a fulfilled human life. The work culture of the past three centuries has been called to account before, but never so insistently as in the 1990s. A first reason for writing this book has been to investigate our present uncertainties about the value of work.

Admittedly, philosophers can sometimes add to the perplexity. Shall I believe Mary Warnock when she tells us 'that even where a job is bad in all sorts of ways, it is better to have it than not, and probably better to work hard at it than less hard'? (Warnock, 1977, p 144). Or Bertrand Russell, who has less time for diligence, having famously dismissed work as 'of two kinds: first, altering the position of matter at or near the earth's surface relatively to other matter; second, telling other people to do so.' (Russell, 1960, p 11).

We won't get far in understanding the value or disvalue of work unless we are a bit more precise – if, sadly, less witty – than Russell in defining the term. I broach this in the next section of Chapter 1. We also need to locate the phenomenon of work in cultural changes that began in the seventeenth century and are still with us. I sketch this in briefly in following sections. Then I home in on schools.

This introduces the book's second theme: education. How far are our fin-de-siecle reassessments of the centrality of work reflected in what goes on in classrooms? Is one function of schoolwork to socialise children into a life committed to the work ethic? But if, as voices in the more general debates proclaim, 'the work society is running out of work' (Dahrendorf, 1982, p.182), what are the implications for schools? Do their present ways of doing things *unfit* young people for their future?

The rest of the book explores in more depth each of the two major themes. Chapter 2 takes us back to ethical brass tacks. Is work, as Marxists and others have claimed, a fundamental human need? Or have we conned ourselves over the centuries into accepting it as such? Should we aim at work which is more meaningful for more people? Or just at less of it all round? Should we be following the enthusiasts, or the sceptics? Among the latter, what attitude should we take to the unemployed surfer on the cover of Philippe van Parijs's (1995) book, shier of work than of the wave about to engulf him?

Chapter 3 leaves this critical appraisal of other philosophers' views on work and presents my own positive account of the place of work in human well-being. Most of the discussion is about the two major types of work I distinguish in the book and which I call 'autonomous' and 'heteronomous'. There is also a section on how work should be distributed.

Clarifying these issues should help us to see how educators might react to different future scenarios – one where the work culture broadly remains in place, another where it is progressively eroded. This leads us into the practical heart of the book, in Chapters 4 and 5. Chapter 4 consists of a reassessment of the nature and purposes of education in relation to work, while Chapter 5 examines how these purposes might be realised in the family, the school and society more generally. It includes a call for a radical reshaping of the school as the work culture has come to know it.

THE MEANING OF WORK

Is there an objective definition of work? The sociologist Keith Grint (1991, p 5) does not think so. It is 'a socially constructed phenomenon without fixed or universal meaning across space and time, but its meanings are delimited by the cultural forms within which it is practised.' (p 46) What I think Grint wants to bring out is that different social groups use the term 'work' in different ways in line with their own values and purposes. He mentions, for instance, the state's division between workers as the 'economically active' who are in paid employment, and non-workers who are 'economically inactive' (p 9). What, then, about women with domestic responsibilities, who on this definition appear 'to spend so long doing nothing'? (ibid.). The economic perspective on work is only one among many.

While Grint is right to point out attempts to delimit the use of the term in this way, it does not follow, as he seems to believe, that one cannot get behind such delimitings and discover some more general meaning. In fact several of Grint's own remarks seem to presuppose this possibility. Consider, for instance, the assumption in the last quotation that women are working at home even though not in paid employment; or his claim that 'work tends to be an activity which transforms nature' (p 7).

Whether his last suggestion is sufficiently general may depend on what is included in 'transforming nature'. It seems closer to the half of Russell's dichotomy about altering the position of matter at or near the earth's surface than to the managerial half to do with telling other people what to do, to say nothing of the work of poets and philosophers.

But at least we can start with Grint's hint that work is a kind of activity. This is surely right. Doing nothing is not working. Doctors may be paid for being on call even though inactive; but we think of this as part of their work because of the readiness for activity if required implicit in the notion of being on call. Similarly, passive enjoyment like dozing in an armchair or lying out in the sun is not work.

If work is a form of activity, not all forms of activity are work. Strolling in the countryside is not; and neither need be listening to a string quartet. Neither agent has to intend the activity to eventuate in some end-product outside the activity itself. In this the activities are unlike making horseshoes or teaching children. One might, of course, say that one strolls in the woods in order to bring about the end-product of an enjoyable stroll; but this is only a restatement of what the activity is and does not introduce an end-product outside it. Listening to quartets *may* be undertaken so as to enlarge one's musical understanding and sensibility – and this does sound like an end-product. But one *may* listen to them also for more intrinsic delights, and if one does so any thought that this is a form of work drops away.

It begins to looks as if, *pace* Grint, there *is* something both 'universal' and 'objective' that we can say about the concept of work, namely that it is a form of activity designed to bring about some end-product outside itself. This end-product might, for instance, be an actual physical object – a sofa or a micro-chip; a service – helping others to learn or cutting their hair; or the solution of some theoretical or practical or artistic problem.

Is this enough? I do not intend to search for a complete definition, assuming any such thing were possible. (If *this* is Grint's target, he may be on the right track.) But we need at least to stress that 'activity' in this context is more than a discrete action. If I help a neighbour to get his car going by lending him my jump leads, this would not normally count as 'work', even though what I do is designed to bring about some end-product – in this case a service rendered. The more I make a practice of helping people with their car problems – for love or for money – the more work-like what I do may become.

My interest in this book is not in a close analysis of the concept of work. I doubt whether one can go much further in a logical direction than we have gone already. Perhaps, indeed, we have already gone too far. My concern is with the place of work in personal flourishing and in education, and for this the roughest of highly general accounts of the concept may well be sufficient. Within this we need to make some further distinctions. Those most helpful to our theme are embodied in the following diagram:

producing X is NOT CHOSEN as major goal	producing X is NOT a major goal	work unwillingly engaged in
		work willingly engaged in
	producing X is a major goal	work unwillingly engaged in
		work willingly engaged in
producing X is CHOSEN as a major goal		

To begin with the left-hand column. The distinction here is between autonomous and heteronomous work. To explain it, I need to bring in the idea of a flourishing human life. As I shall be using the term, a life can be said to be more flourishing, that is, is higher on a scale of well-being, the more the agent's major goals in life are fulfilled. By 'major goals' I have in mind those which are more important to the individual over his or her lifetime as a whole in a personal hierarchy of importance. Among other things, I like doing crosswords and eating biscuits. But there are things that mean more to me, like intimate relationships, thinking about philosophy or enjoying natural beauty. I could give up the two former, but not the three latter. They are among my major goals. Insofar as I am able to pursue them my well-being is enhanced. Should so many things crowd into my life as to leave me no time to do these things, it would be seriously diminished.

The notion of a life of greater or lesser well-being applies to all human beings and perhaps some animals also – for a cat can have major goals like resting in comfort, hunting, eating when hungry, being made a fuss of; and in any particular cat's life these goals may be satisfied to a greater or lesser extent. Among human beings, there are often quite large differences as to how far the goals are self-chosen and how far they are imposed from the outside – by custom, for instance, or religious or political leaders. This gives us a distinction, vital to the whole argument of this book, between autonomous and non-autonomous well-being. Non-autonomous tribesmen have major goals ascribed to them by custom, like being a good father or warrior, which they might with luck achieve or without luck fail to do so. In our own society we take it for granted that people will by and large choose their own most important goals and that their kind of well-being depends on success in their pursuit.

To come back now to the left-hand column. Autonomous work is a form of activity whose end-product (X) is chosen as such as a major goal of an autonomous agent. Imagine someone who chooses teaching, caring for the sick or journalism in this way, who not merely chooses it as the best option given that they have to earn a living, but as something which they would prefer to do even if they did not have to earn a living. This would be an example of autonomous work *par excellence*. So would voluntary work in an Oxfam shop. Other work is heteronomous, that is, its end-product is not chosen as a major goal, but is in some way unavoidable or required of one.

This brings us to the middle column. The distinction now is between work where it is one of one's major goals to produce end-product X and work where this is not the case. The former type covers autonomous work, as just defined, but also includes some kinds of heteronomous work. Imagine a peasant farmer in a traditional society. He has not chosen to become a peasant. In his society such autonomous possibilities are unknown: he is simply doing what his fore-fathers have always done, doing what is expected of him. High among his most cherished goals, we can assume, is providing adequate food, clothing and shelter for his family. Another example, literally closer to home, would be work which women have traditionally done in the shape of housework, shopping, childcare – given that they do this not, as many women do, through autonomous choice in preference to other options, but simply because this is expected of them. I shall call work of this general kind, that is where X is one's major goal, whether autonomously chosen or not, 'personally significant' work. (This is to be taken as useful shorthand, not carrying further connotations.)

But in other kinds of heteronomous work the end-product does not have such significance to the worker. Imagine a slave in a stone quarry; or a company manager working for a biscuit firm who, if the pay were equally good, might one day find herself in cement. 'Personally non-significant' work ranges from cases where the 'X' is repulsive from the viewpoint of one's major goals, as with the slave, through to milder negative attitudes: towards making lemon puffs and garibaldis, for instance, or settling for school teaching when one knows one is really a writer. Personal priorities can change, of course. People stumble into teaching and then find it highly fulfilling. Work initially classifiable as 'person-ally non-significant' can in time cross categories.

I have no statistics, but would judge that a very large proportion of work in a modern society like Britain is personally non-significant. This applies to managerial and non-managerial work alike. In the light of this, perhaps this cat-egory is close to the Marxist notion of 'alienated labour'. I prefer not to use that concept, however, because of the complex theoretical assumptions it carries. 'Personally non-significant', for all its aesthetic demerits as a term, is at least reasonably precise.

Let me turn to the third column. This introduces a distinction between work willingly and unwillingly engaged in, bearing in mind that there is no sharp dichotomy, only a continuum, between the two. We are now concerned not with the product, but the process – with whether the activity itself is appealing or unappealing. Autonomous work may be painful – as philosophis-ing was for Wittgenstein; but since it is directed to end-products to which one has chosen to give very high priority, we can expect a high commitment, too, to tasks leading to these goals. Some non-autonomous, but personally signifi-cant, work is also willingly undertaken: if all is going well for them, the peasant farmer or traditional housewife and mother may enjoy their day-to-day tasks. With odds more against them, other farmers or housewives may find their lives misery.

The willingness-unwillingness dimension is especially important for 'personally non-significant' work. Toiling in a Siberian mine is hell; filling Tesco shelves is usually plain boring; driving a minicab can be more interesting at times; while organising others to produce buttons, car exhausts, travel insurance and other goods of no major personal significance to one can often be highly enjoyable – and all the more so as salaries, pension rights, free time, congenial company, social recognition and other benefits increase.

The attractiveness of work at the pleasanter end of the continuum explains why autonomous agents often choose it as a major goal despite its personal non-significance. Remember we are not here talking about autonomous *work*. There is a vital difference between *autonomous work* and *autonomous agency in work*. For the autonomous worker, the end-product is all-important and irreplaceable; but a person can choose autonomously to work in a stock-brokers' firm even though helping others towards the best share deals is not a major goal but only a replaceable instrument to attain wealth, respect, good company and other advantages. It is the ultimate benefits towards which this is a means which constitute the agent's major goals, not this service in itself.

Remember, too, that autonomy itself lies on a continuum, in that some people are more autonomous than others: they are better equipped to make choices, have more options available to them, and so on. Not only stock-brokers and senior company executives have a place on the continuum, but also people who choose to become gardeners in preference to factory-workers, or secretaries in a university rather than in business. Once again, it is the attractiveness of their working conditions which lies closer than the product itself to the autonomous agent's major goals.

So much for the diagram. The further significance of all the various distinctions will be revealed as the whole argument unrolls. For the moment, I'd like to focus again on the first column, on the distinction between autonomous and heteronomous work. The latter is constrained in a way the former is not since the end-product is not chosen as one of one's major goals: the work is in some sense something one has to do, like it or not. This element of constraint or necessity is often present in accounts of what work *in general* involves. It comes out in Keith Grint's remark that 'in some senses work is the opposite of leisure: it is something we have to do, something we may prefer not to do and something we tend to get paid for.' (op. cit., p 11). We find it, too, in Ralf Dahrendorf's (1982, p 183) distinction between 'work' and 'activity'. 'Work is human action which is heteronomous, imposed by external needs, be they needs of survival or of power. Activity, on the other hand, is human action which is freely chosen, which offers opportunities for self-expression, which carries satisfaction within itself, which is autonomous.'

It is not surprising that 'work' tends to get defined in a way which excludes what I have called 'autonomous work' (which in Dahrendorf becomes a form of 'activity'). So little of the work that has ever been done in human history has been autonomous; so little, too, of the work done in the world today; so little in contemporary Britain. For nearly everyone, work is and has always been something unavoidable, something which one has to do for one reason or another. This external constraint can take different forms. For slaves, it has been fear of chastisement; for Puritan businessmen, duty to God; while most of those who take on paid employment are obliged to do so in order to have food, clothing and other necessities. (The customary connexion between 'work' and 'external constraint' is preserved, in an extended or perhaps metaphorical sense, in the notion of a pregnant woman going into 'labour' to produce a baby. The constraint here is a necessity of nature.)

Constrained, or heteronomous, work includes much more than paid employment, slavery, and Puritan self-employment. For one thing, it can include being unemployed. Many people on the dole are not there by preference and are obliged to spend a large part of their time making applications for jobs and providing evidence of diligence in this regard. They are not productive in the way that employed workers produce goods and services, but they can still be busily producing documentation. Heteronomous work can also include much unpaid housework, decorating, gardening, shopping for basics, car maintenance, care of young children and care of the sick or elderly. That is, once again, where people do not do these things by choice, but are obliged to do them for some reason or other: there is no one else; they can't afford paid help; they have family obligations.

It can also cover activities in which children are obliged to take part in compulsory school classes. Whether or not they enjoy their lessons is not a relevant consideration: they still have to attend them, like it or not, just as many in paid employment like what they are doing but still need the money, come what may. True, the children, even the most willing, are more constrained than the adults, in that although the latter need a paid job, they do not have to have one in a specific area, like road-building or butchering, while pupils at school normally cannot avoid studying geography, French or chemistry – and at times fixed by others. Obligatory school activities count as 'work', i.e. 'schoolwork', where there is some kind of end-product in prospect – an essay, for example, a drawing, or a solution to a problem in mathematics. Beyond this kind of end-product, teachers typically have further intentions in mind, connected with their wider educational aims. Sometimes these are known to the pupil, sometimes not – as where a child does not realise that the work she is being asked to do is intended to reinforce dispositions like accuracy or religious commitment, benevolence, or obedience to authority. Sometimes apparently pointless classroom activities may have such hidden aims: more than one educational system across the millenia has discerned in 'mindless' rote-learning a means of inducing unquestioning obedience.

Incidentally, this last point reminds us, if we needed reminding, that not all work is directed towards *palpably useful* end-products like furniture, beer and yoga tuition. Soldiers on basic training have been known to be kept busy, in the absence of more pressing tasks, by being made to cut the grass around their huts with scissors. Does 'work' then also cover pointless, as well as obviously useful, production? It is not easy to tell from an example like this: the soldiers might be viewed as providing a service to their military masters in the shape of a greater readiness to do whatever might be required of them, no questions asked. There may be a parallel with apparently pointless classroom activities, as we have just seen. Perhaps, after all, examples of purely pointless production might be hard to find.

'Work' in the more limited sense, as constrained activity, also has application beyond human beings. Workhorses and oxen pull carts and ploughs. Even machines can be accommodated, if we are willing to abstract from the animal-orientated connotations of 'constraint' and 'activity' and subsume these under still wider categories such as 'unavoidability' and 'motion'. A washing machine, once turned on and 'in working order', will do what is necessary to make towels clean: it cannot help getting through its programme, its mechanism and the laws of nature being what they are.

The notion can also be extended in another dimension. Beyond the point where the notion of constraint proper becomes inapplicable, it might still be appropriate to use the wider category, under which 'constraint' fits, of putting pressure on a person to get them to do something. Given this extension, we can embrace under 'work' activities arising from outside pressuring, not least of consumers. The sign outside a farm shop in Hertfordshire 'Customers wanted: no experience necessary' is good fun, but it prompts the idea that from the viewpoint of the seller, the buyer can be seen as performing a service. The more that consumers can be persuaded to engage in activities leading to such an end-product, the more they take on the characteristics of workers. Think of supermarkets: not only has the customer been induced to take on the labours of the old small shop assistant in removing goods from shelves, loading and unloading them: in the course of all this, she is serving Tesco or Safeway by responding to their psychological seductions and being tempted to impulse-buy in every other aisle. The invention of shopping trolleys, as Thomas Sutcliffe wrote in a review of a recent television series on 'Shopping', was 'a stroke of genius, instantly increasing the productivity of busy shoppers, who had, quite unwittingly, volunteered for unpaid work in the temples of consumption' (*The Independent*, 11 July 1995, Section Two, p 24).

The conventional link between work and constraint can even be extended to the sphere of what would normally be taken to be autonomous work, from which I have so far disassociated it. It is sometimes said of great artists and thinkers that they are 'driven by their daemon', the implication being that it is not their own will which directs them, but some alien force.

In all these various ways, 'work' is commonly thought of as something unavoidable, constrained, necessary. This is an important fact, as we shall now see. At the same time, we need to remember that the most general concept of work – to do with activity designed to generate an end-product – goes beyond this, embracing also autonomous work. This creates a minor terminological difficulty for me in the rest of this paper, since sometimes I shall be wanting to speak of 'work' in the wider sense and sometimes in the narrower. Rather than go in for subscripts, italics or other devices which oblige readers to leaf back at intervals to remind themselves of how to interpret them, I hope the context should make things clear.

It may be helpful to recapitulate the main distinctions made in this section, since they will all be put to use later. The basic concept underpinning the book's main argument is *activity*. Work is one form of activity, that is, activity designed to eventuate in some end-product – as distinct, for instance, from activity pursued for intrinsic reasons. Work is in principle either autonomous or heteronomous (although there may not be a sharp line between these in practice). People engage in autonomous work when [a] they are self-directed in the conduct of their lives, and [b] the end-product is something of great significance in their personal vision of how they wish to live. Very few people in the history of the world, or, indeed, alive today, have been able to engage in much, if any, autonomous work. Nearly all work has been heteronomous. It is something which the worker has been constrained to do for some reason. *Some* heteronomous work, like *all* autonomous work, has been of personal significance to the agent. But again, a great deal of it, perhaps nearly all of it, has not been. Even personally non-significant work – undertaken, perhaps, simply to earn a living – can be very enjoyable. Many people in our kind of culture find it the more attractive the more opportunities it provides for self-direction rather than subordination to others' commands. Although it makes good sense, as many people do, to call this kind of work 'autonomous', it is crucial to the book's whole argument that this be distinguished from autonomous work as defined earlier in this paragraph. Managers in insurance firms may have plenty of scope in the way they organise their work, but few of them are as personally attached to their professional end-products as teachers, nurses and artists are to theirs. In the terminology I shall use, *autonomy in work* is not to be conflated with *autonomous work* as such. I underline this point for reasons which will become clearer in the sequel.

THE WORK CULTURE

The centrality of work

As we have seen, work in the narrower sense, work as heteronomous, takes many forms. It covers virtually all paid employment – all, that is, except that which a person would take on even if unpaid, much housework and house maintenance, shopping, child care, schoolwork and even activities flowing from being unemployed. Until very recently – the last few years – the striking fact about work has been that it has filled nearly all our lives. Only pre-school children and some retired adults have escaped its demands. Broadly speaking, we have lived to work. This has been so both over a lifetime and, more microscopically, from day to day. For virtually all of us each day has been nearly completely taken up either with work or with what is necessary to work effectively – sleep, eating, washing, eliminating, relaxation, recreation.

The last few years have brought massive changes in employment patterns, with nearly 30 per cent of the working population now either officially unemployed or otherwise economically inactive (Hutton 1995, p 106). Although work does not in fact fill these people's lives as it fills most people's, the *social ideal* of a life devoted to work is much more universal, the unemployed who dream of a job and feel demeaned and worthless without one being more under its spell than many in work.

The rival ideal to a work society over the last century has been that of a leisure society, in which work plays a smaller and smaller part. Some see progress towards this as inevitable. But it is easy to be mistaken or confused about this. One source of error may be a Whiggish attitude to the Industrial Revolution and its aftermath to date: we know that working hours (in the narrow sense of 'paid employment') are far less now than in the nineteenth century and we may assume that this process is irreversible. As a matter of historical fact, however, it seems that the efforts of nineteenth- and early twentieth-century reformers to reduce working hours lost steam after the middle of this century. As Witold Rybczinski (1991, p 216) has shown, while in 1948 13 per cent of Americans worked more than 49 hours a week, by 1979 this had increased to 18 per cent, and by 1989 to 24 per cent. More generally, most Americans had 9.6 hours less free time in 1988 than in 1973. British evidence is similar. Polly Toynbee writes that 'since the turn of the century, the story of working hours has been one of a steady and decent reduction. This stopped in the early Seventies, and, during the Eighties, the managerial/professional group, who now form a third of the workforce, actually added two more hours to their working week in unpaid overtime.' (*The Independent*,10 June 1995, Magazine Section, p 14). According to a recent report by the TUC, 'the number of people working "excessive" hours has grown significantly over the past decade, with one in five workers now on a 50-hour week' (*The Independent*,17 May 1995). As the numbers of unemployed grow at one end, those who still have full-time jobs can find themselves working harder than ever.

I described the ideal of a leisure society as *opposed* to the ideal of a work society. But in the way that the term 'leisure' tends to be used today, this is not true without qualification. 'Leisure' tends to mean 'free time', that is, time not spent in paid employment. Our understanding of leisure is dependent, if only negatively, on the notion of work. In addition, even though leisure lies beyond paid *employment,*this does not mean that it excludes heteronomous work – in that one may be constrained to use some of one's free time for activities like shopping or housework.

Other ingredients of leisure are work-dependent, in that work makes demands on one in one's time away from it. One has to sleep, eat and wash. One also needs recreation. People work better if they have time off – evenings, weekends, holidays – in which they can relax, take exercise, socialise and pursue other interests. This is true of all work, autonomous as well as heteronomous.

This contemporary concept of leisure is different from that of the Greeks, discussed especially by Aristotle. The latter is logically linked to the notion of the intrinsically good life for human beings (*eudaimonia*). To possess leisure is to engage in those activities which constitute such a life. In Aristotle's treatment of the topic in *Nicomachean Ethics* Book 10 the defining such activity is contemplation, but on other views of human flourishing, 'leisure' could be differently, perhaps more generously, conceived (Telfer 1987). Unlike the modern conception, the classical notion is not defined in terms of work, but in terms of the good life. At the same time, the ancient leisure society rested materially, if not conceptually, on a work society – of slaves.

Let us return to the main point. We have inherited the notion that work, largely heteronomous work, should be central to our lives. Where it is not, we see this as a failure of the system, as something to be put right by better policies of 'full employment'. We attach value to leisure also, but mainly as a necessary adjunct of work. More radical notions of a leisure society in either the modern sense of a massive liberation from work or in the classical sense built around positive, rather than negative, ideals may get high ratings among some hippyish inhabitants of Glastonbury or Hebden Bridge; but have fired few others.

The background to centrality

The doctrine of work's centrality has been deeply rooted in British culture for more than three hundred years. Politically it has always been the dominant ideology of all parties, from socialists through to free marketeers.

In socialism it has been the *dominant* view, but not the only one. I have already mentioned the Marxist tradition. As Arendt points out, Marx's attitude towards labour is equivocal. On the one hand, labour is an 'eternal necessity'; on the other, the post-revolution 'realm of freedom begins only where labour determined through want and external utility ceases' (Arendt 1958, p 90). A similar tension runs through British Labour Party thinking up to our own times: on the one hand, the adulation of 'labour' in the very title of the party, the old Clause 4's concentration on 'workers by hand or by brain', the unquestioned attachment to 'full employment'; on the other – and not nearly so prominent – the dream of a society without unwelcome toil, where human beings are free to lead lives of their own choosing.

It is well known that British Labour Party thinking has been influenced by

Christianity as much as by Marxism. A key influence in British Christianity in the last four hundred years has been the Puritan movement of the seventeenth century with its revolutionary conception of the place of work in human well-being. (Indeed, via Locke, it contributed to Marx's views about work.) The 'Puritan work ethic' has helped to shape not only British Christianity and British socialism: as Tawney (1926), Anthony (1977, ch 2) and others have shown, it played a large part in the rise of capitalism, in Britain, elsewhere in Europe, North America, and now the world over.

Tawney describes the change in the conception of the religious life which seventeenth century Puritanism brought with it: a rejection of the earlier monastic ideal of contemplation in favour of full involvement in the everyday life of business. Contemplation came to be seen as self-indulgence; spiritual victories were won 'not in the cloister, but on the battlefield, in the counting house and in the market'. Life was to be lived in the pursuit of one's particular calling, which was at the same time both spiritual and temporal. Through this notion of one's divinely-appointed vocation, work came to be the central element in a holy life, a lifelong enterprise transcending mere isolated good works. It now became a spiritual end, in which the soul could find health – 'a duty long after it has ceased to be a material necessity'. This was an ideal of life 'opposed to luxury, unrestrained pleasure, personal extravagance, also excessive devotion to friends and relations'. It was also an ideal applicable to every social station. The poor were seen as damned in the next world. Poverty was something to be avoided on spiritual grounds, even if it meant a life of hard physical toil: 'it were better to beat down the body and to keep it in subjection by a laborious calling, than through luxury to become a castaway'. (A view more colourfully expressed than, but curiously reminiscent of, Mary Warnock's observation above). As for the rich, they are 'no more excused from work than the poor, though they may rightly use their riches to select some occupation specially serviceable to others' (ibid.). In general, 'not sufficiency to the needs of daily life, but limitless increase and expansion, became the goal of the Christian's efforts', an appetite for gain now being seen as a virtue rather than a vice, in contrast with the older idea of usury as a sin. (References in this paragraph are to Tawney (1926) pp 230, 240–246, 265).

More recently than Tawney, Charles Taylor (1989, Part III) has explored similar territory. For him the Puritan revolution was an 'affirmation of ordinary life', meaning by the latter 'those aspects of human life concerned with production and reproduction, that is, labour, the making of things needed for life, and our life as sexual beings, including marriage and the family' (p 211). He also stresses its link with science and technology, arguing that 'the Puritan theology of work and ordinary life provided a hospitable environment for the scientific revolution' (p 230).

The overwhelmingly secular society that Britain now is is still affected to its core by the wraiths of these ancient religious beliefs. At times in British history they have won through to especial prominence – in Victorian times, for instance, and during our own lives in the Thatcherite revolution of the 1980s. Although he himself does not point out the parallel, Taylor's picture of the Puritan elevation of ordinary life reminds one irresistibly of Thatcherism: the same emphasis on business virtues, on family values, on technological progress through the application of science. Even the seventeenth century reversal of the monastic ideal has its resonances in the Thatcherite demotion of the universities.

Enjoying one's work

Heteronomous work occupies most of most people's waking hours. It is the central feature of their lives, about which other things pivot. Since most of it not only is externally constrained, but also has end-products of no personal significance, one would expect those who have to do it to prefer not to do it, given that they were not financially disadvantaged. Very often, of course, this is so. But, equally, very often not. Most people enjoy their jobs; some, indeed, are 'workaholics'. How can this be explained?

Some kinds of external constraint are compatible with enjoyment, others not. It is hard to see how anyone could enjoy working in a Nazi slave labour camp, but a Puritan businessman no doubt willingly accepted his imposed duty to labour. He has his counterparts today. If they have no religious obligations, they may still be powered by obligations of a moral sort. Many of those who opt for careers in teaching, health care, the police and other forms of public service see their work under this aspect: they may feel it to be their moral duty to do what they can to relieve sickness or ignorance, to uphold the law and so on.

Other people enjoy their jobs to different degrees, despite the element of constraint, and even though they are not driven by a sense of religious or moral obligation. What has happened in many cases is that workers themselves or employers short of workers have built all sorts of congenial features into heteronomous and personally non-significant jobs. There is an unspoken compromise between necessity and personal fulfilment. Among ingredients of the latter, at least for many people, are: social recognition; company; the opportunity to cooperate with others in activities with shared ends; income well beyond subsistence level; security; a comfortable environment; time to do what one wants; opportunities for the exercise of autonomy. All these things can be and are incorporated into jobs – in the shape of such things as marks of high status, power over subordinates, being part of a team, high salaries and pension packages; air-conditioned workplaces; tea-breaks; generous leave; wide scope for decision-making. A 'good job', as popularly understood, is one which has more of these kinds of advantages. As we know, people compete for the 'better' jobs, both over the whole range and in sub-ranges of the whole. These jobs may not give them autonomous work as earlier defined. Workers may still spend their lives sorting out insurance claims or making three-pin plugs where producing these things is far from their ideal picture of how to lead their lives. Autonomous work is, as we have said, different from autonomy *in* work (see above). Those in the better of the best jobs may have the latter in plenty.

Competing for good jobs seems to me an understandable and intelligent way of coping with the centrality of work in our culture while at the same time trying to make one's life as satisfying as possible. It is easy to see how those who get the 'better' jobs can become workaholics. We do not have to put such addiction down to Puritan or moral zeal, although this may well account for some of it. Given that the process-features of one's job, if not its products, enable one to satisfy one's major goals in life, this would seem to be a very fulfilling way of spending one's time.

It may be that the British, perhaps because of their lengthier experience of industrialised society, have woven this strand more firmly into their culture than other nations. According to a recent British Social Attitudes survey, 74 per cent of British workers said that they would still prefer a paid job even if they had enough money without (Toynbee, 1995). A passage from Ralf Dahrendorf's (1982) *On Britain* is also revealing:

> When Prince Philip, perhaps in a slightly unguarded moment, said in an interview that he did not understand why people on the one hand wanted more leisure, and on the other hand complained about unemployment, he made a valid, but also a rather un-British point. Of course, trade unions talk about shorter working hours; but the British do not necessarily want more leisure, however much they like their races and fishing and the rest. They are quite happy to spend the major part of their waking hours on their jobs. The notion of office workers starting at 7.30 in the morning, and going home at 3.30 or 4 o'clock in the afternoon, or factory workers starting at 6.30 and going home at 2.30 or 3 o'clock in order to do other things, is by no means as general as it is on the Continent or in the United States. For one thing, many people do not like to start work at 7.30, let alone at 6.30 in the morning. Leisure still means evenings, weekends, holidays; it is a small and separate part of everyday life.
>
> The other side of this picture is that one lives at work, that is to say, one does not go to work in order to work, but in order to spend an agreeable day. This is an overstatement, of course, but worth pursuing for a moment. There are local councils which have so-called Works Departments, the only function of which seems to be to keep people on the payroll. If they are sent to do something, it is pathetic to watch them. Council workers are highly visible, though hardly typical. Yet there are other cases in point. Tea breaks, for example, are a British invention. And here as elsewhere, the classes meet in a peculiar fashion. The equivalent of the tea break with directors or professional people is drinks before lunch; the advantage they have over tea-drinking workers is that the drinks are in fact followed by a luncheon as well. Whereas working people stretch their work so that it begins to look like leisure, managers and professional people constrain their leisure so that it has at least the appearance of work.

Overstatements apart, any foreigner who watches the British at work cannot help being amazed at their leisurely pace. ... This, incidentally, is not said with any critical intention. What we are describing is one of the reasons for the very pleasantness of life in Britain which is so widely, and so rightly, admired.

EDUCATION AND THE WORK CULTURE

What place does the education system have in a society premised, like the British, on the centrality of (heteronomous) work? We should reject one familiar way of thinking about this. It is misleading to see schools as autonomous vis-à-vis 'the world of work' in the sense that it is still an open question whether or not they should be preparing pupils for this or for something else, for leisure, perhaps, or personal fulfilment. As soon as they begin compulsory schooling pupils are as much involved in work as lorry-drivers or mothers looking after children. They are constrained to engage in activities directed to some end-product or other whether they want this or not. For them as much as for adults, heteronomous work comes to be the central feature of their lives, the arrival of homework in increasing amounts with the transition to secondary school and the preparation for public examinations hard on its heels powerfully reinforcing this.

Part of Conservative educational policy since 1979 has been to make schools more work-like. Even though children are obliged to come to school, this does not automatically mean they get involved in work. The latter requires not just any kind of activity, but activity – of an effortful sort – directed towards end-products. Some compulsory school activities may lack this feature, whether through design, at the hand of some kinds of 'child-centred' teachers, for instance, or unintentionally, through lax classroom control. British government policy has been directed against teachers – real or imaginary – in both categories. The coming of the National Curriculum has required all teachers to set clear, assessable objectives across the board.

If I am right in claiming that, as things are now, work is central to most people's lives as a day-to-day reality – and to nearly everybody's as a social ideal, it would not be surprising if schools and those who control their curricula made work-related aims central to their thinking. On any reasonable account of education, its aims should fit rather than unfit young people for adult life. Philosophers and others less in gear with social realities may argue that education should have nothing or little to do with work – that its proper remit is intrinsically valuable activities, democratic citizenship, or self-realisation; but unless it is made very clear how these things can be accommodated to lives unavoidably dominated by work, their monographs risk confinement to the shelves of education libraries, lacking any influence on policy.

By and large, schools *do* aim at preparing pupils for a life of adult work.

Perhaps their greatest contribution is in habituation – in involving pupils in work from the age of five (or earlier) and making this progressively more dominant in their lives between five and sixteen or eighteen. When they leave school, their minds are – ideally, at least – set firmly in the work ethos. More than that: seeing that schoolwork is often about subject-matter remote from young people's lives and interests, it can be a particularly useful device to prepare them for the personally non-significant work which most will be doing as adults. A second form of preparation is in equipping students, where suitable, with the qualifications needed for entry into 'better' jobs. A third is in arranging the curriculum, and priorities within it, to fit the demands of adult work, highlighting literacy, numeracy, science and technology.

A large part of the school's job is to *motivate* children not only to want to work but also to accept the dominant place of work in their future lives. *Prima facie,*as we have seen, heteronomous work as externally constrained activity – especially where it has no personal significance for one – goes against the grain: people, not least children, do not like having to do what they would otherwise prefer not to do. What kinds of motivational appeals can schools make?

One with its origins in Puritanism could be to one's sense of duty, either religious or moral. Schoolwork, as much as a later vocation, could be presented as 'God's work'. Perhaps Fred Clarke (1923, p 2) had something like this in mind when he wrote 'the ultimate reason for teaching Long Division to little Johnny is that he is an immortal soul' – although whether he saw this reason for teaching mathematics as a reason employable to motivate little Johnny to learn it is unclear. Whatever the truth here, religious motivation is likely to be less in evidence today than when Clarke was writing – and far less than in the nineteenth century. The issue is an empirical one and would need empirical investigation.

As would the question how far teachers and parents these days rely on an appeal to *moral* duty, where this is detached from religious notions. Perhaps this is not often presented to children very explicitly. From impressionistic evidence, it would seem that pupils often carry out the tasks they are set at school out of some vague, unreflective feeling that this is what they should do or that classmates who fail to perform them are doing something not merely against their own interests but also something wrong.

Referring to religious or moral duty as a source of motivation is only half the story, for the obvious thought arises: how are children motivated to do their duty?

A second motivational appeal that educators can make is to self-interest. In some cases this may answer the question just raised: doing one's duty may lead to rewards, on earth or in an afterlife; or it may keep one safe from penalties. But heteronomous work can also be presented as enjoyable in itself. This can be viewed in two contexts. If we want to portray *adult* work to children in a favourable light, this is easier the more personal advantages it contains, that is, the 'better' a job it is. The other context is *school* work. Here, too, the more features it has which pupils already find desirable, the more the issue of motivation evaporates. To some extent these features can overlap with those prized in adult work: social recognition, company, cooperating with others on common tasks, opportunities for the exercise of autonomy. In other ways there will be divergences: schoolwork does not generate a high income or power over others; on the other hand, children can get drawn into it for its intrinsic delights (so that what may have been personally non-significant becomes of absorbing interest) – something harder to imagine in most workplaces. Insofar as there *is* an overlap, this fact makes it all the easier to see how schoolwork is continuous with adult-work and can prepare the way for it – this is true at least as far as 'better' jobs go: children can get used at school to work which offers recognition, social interaction, autonomy etc and expect to find these in the work they do as adults. This still leaves the less desirable jobs, the ones which erode rather than subserve personal well-being. The more schoolwork matches 'better' adult jobs, the harder it becomes for those who do not succeed in getting one of these 'better' jobs to accommodate themselves to a 'worse' one. Not only are there the disadvantages intrinsic to the job itself, there is also the further pain caused by disappointed expectations.

Still assuming the centrality of heteronomous work in society, it would seem to follow that schools which encourage recognition and autonomy would find it easier to operate against the background of a social policy that sought to eliminate the more 'undesirable' forms of work. If the status quo policy were maintained, it is hard to see what schools could do to motivate future workers in the 'worse' jobs. I am assuming that we are ruling out, on grounds of cruelty, getting children likely to find themselves in such jobs to have such low self-esteem that they come to think that these are all they are fit for. This might *come about*, of course, with no such intention on teachers' parts but as a by-product of wider institutional structures. Some people have seen the assessment system associated with the National Curriculum in this light.

NOTES

1. Paul Vallely, *The Independent*, 27 May 1995.
2. *The Independent*, 12 April 1996.
3. 'No rest for the British', *The Independent on Sunday*, 4 August 1996. On comparisons with the Continent, the article states that in Britain 'between 1983 and 1991 the average working week for full-time employees in the service sector went up from 41.9 hours to 43.1 hours, but fell from 40.3 hours to 40 hours in the rest of Europe'
4. Obituary in *The Independent*, 6 July 1995.
5. *The Independent*, 23 June 1996.

TWO

Philosophers at work on work

INTRODUCTION

'Ten years ago' Tom Hodgkinson wrote recently in *The Guardian*, 'the conversation at twenty-something parties generally centred around careers. Those without work would say: "I must get a job." Those unhappy in their work would say: "I must get a new job." At such parties now, the aspirations are very different. I have met so many people in the last year – with jobs and without – who have said: "What I want is regular employment for two or three days a week. That would give me a basic income to pursue my own projects." ' (*The Guardian*, 16 May 1995).

As suggested in Chapter 1, we live in a three-hundred-year-old culture which has made work – in effect, mainly heteronomous work – the chief ingredient of a worthwhile life. Is this culture coming to an end? Is the doctrine of work loosening its hold over us? How typical are Tom Hodgkinson and his fellow party-goers?

If we knew the answers to these questions, we would be in a better position to know whether the education system needs reshaping for what Anthony Giddens (1995) has called a 'post-productivist' world. As a philosopher, and neither an empirical sociologist nor a prophet, I have no answers. But what my discipline *can* do is examine the fundamental assumptions of the work culture and see if they stand up to logical and ethical scrutiny. If they do, 'productivism' would be worth retaining, whatever new cohorts of twenty-somethings might say about it. If they do not, philosophy itself may play some part, through disseminating this conclusion, in the erosion of the old order.

I said in Chapter 1 that the doctrine of work's centrality has belonged to several traditions of thought over the last three or four centuries – Christian, socialist and capitalist. An idea powerful enough to unite forces often otherwise at loggerheads must have entrenched itself deeply in institutional life – and so indeed it did. Consider nineteenth-century Britain, with its puritan-spirited churches, its workhouses and laws against vagrancy, its elementary schools inducting children into a regime of diligence. Or its twentieth-century successor, with its selective education systems more carefully attuned to a range of employment needs, its reverence for full employment, its welfare state pivoting on benefits for those debarred by youth, illness, old age or worklessness from life's central activity.

That work *has been* at the heart of our social and personal life there is no gainsaying. The philosophical question is: *should it be?*

To answer this, we need to look at arguments in favour of its importance. At the social level, there is in one sense no doubt of this. If no one worked, we would lack the wherewithal not only of a civilised existence, but of *any* existence. I take this as read. The claim is a very general one: all it says is that social life could not go on without work. It says nothing about how much work there should be and of what sort, or who should undertake it. The 'doctrine of work' associated with our work culture goes further than the banal proposition that some sort of work by somebody or other is socially necessary. It ties work to *personal* salvation or, in a variant more agreeable to a secular age, *personal* fulfilment. Work, it tells us, work to which we cleave either through religious or moral duty, or from economic necessity, should be the cornerstone of our existence.

For the rest of this book I shall be exploring the place of work in *individuals'* lives and in their upbringing. Some of the issues that this raises will not detain me long. The religious notion, for instance, so powerful in the creation of the work culture, that a life of hard work is a sign of salvation. Its presupposed belief in the existence of God and of an afterlife is something I do not share. For that reason, which may or may not be thought adequate, I shall ignore it.

Religion aside, how could one ever hope to show that work should be at the core of our being? If nearly all work is heteronomous, how can something we are obliged, required or forced to do be of such vital significance to us?

In Chapter 2 I consider what light some modern philosophers have cast on the worthwhileness of work. I put them in four groups. First, those who argue that work is a basic human need. Secondly, those who press for meaningful work for all on other grounds. The third section discusses Hannah Arendt and her well-known distinction between work and labour; while the fourth looks at the sceptics: these turn their back on the work culture, unlike thinkers in the first two groups, who in some sense take it as read.

WORK AND HUMAN NATURE

As we shall see below, a number of contemporary philosophical accounts of work base the positive value which they attach to it on an appeal to human nature. In some, Norman and Sayers, for instance, work, or 'meaningful work', appears as a basic human *need*, that is, as something which every human being requires if he or she is to survive or to lead a flourishing life. Others, like Attfield, link work with 'the human *essence*', holding that 'an essential capacity of human beings is the capacity for meaningful work' (Attfield 1984, p 148).

Needs-talk and essence-talk come in these cases to very much the same thing. Both sets of writers take work/meaningful work/the capacity for meaningful work to be an ineluctable (i.e. necessary or essential) feature of human existence or well-being. Both kinds of discourse are directly traceable back to Marx.

Marx

Among the many passages in which Marx writes about work and its place in human life, two accounts are of particular relevance. The first is about human beings' essential capacities as tool-using or tool-making animals, the second about work as a 'prime need of life' in a communist society.

According to one interpretation of a passage from *The German Ideology* (Marx and Engels 1965), Marx held that what distinguishes men from other animals is not consciousness or religion, but the fact that they produce their own means of subsistence by the use of tools. Elsewhere, Marx approvingly mentions Franklin's view of man as a 'tool-making animal' (*Capital* I, p 179). Both these claims about human uniqueness are false according to Benjamin Beck's *Animal Tool Behaviour*, cited by Jon Elster (1985, pp 64–66). Even if they were true, however, it is hard to see what ethical recommendations would follow from them, given the familiar problem of arguing from empirical fact to evaluative conclusions. In particular, they would lend no support to any claim that work must be a *central* element in human flourishing.

As Elster (1985, p 84) also shows, Marx's views on the place of work in a communist society are ambiguous and at first sight contradictory. Marx writes [1] that work 'will become a prime need of life'; [2] that work will become largely superfluous owing to the automation of production: man 'steps to the side of the production process instead of being its chief actor'; and [3] that, while work, as found in 'the realm of necessity', is unavoidable, man will realise himself in 'the true realm of freedom' which lies beyond this.

Elster suggests that these accounts can be rendered mutually compatible if one interprets Marx as saying that the work which will be a prime need is engagement in some kind of creative activity. Industrial work as we know it will wither away, although some drudgery will continue to exist, at least for some people.

A central issue is whether there are good grounds in support of the claim that work, in the shape of creative activity, is a prime human need. Elster equates it with the thesis of 'the priority of creation over consumption, of activity over passivity' (p 85). He sees a possible inconsistency in this. Given that creation is of objects – artefacts, works of art, theories, etc – for other people to engage with, creation is parasitic on consumption. 'To put the matter starkly: in a society entirely made up of active, creative individuals nobody would be bothered to read, watch or otherwise enjoy what others are producing, except to learn from them.' (p 87).

But is there really an inconsistency here? To say that creative activity is a prime need is not to say that individuals would spend all or even most of their time on it, or that they would not want to do anything else. It only means that human beings could not flourish unless they took part in creative activities and did so in a major way. It might equally be true that the consumption of creative activities is a major human need, perhaps even a 'prime need' on a par with creation. Even though creation is parasitic on consumption, this does nothing to show that the latter could not count as a prime need.

Even so, there does seem to be a certain arbitrariness in Marx's position. If creative work is indeed a need – leave aside a prime one, then what makes it necessary to our flourishing? Elster's equation of it with activity as contrasted with passivity or consumption misses the target. For not all activity is creative activity. Playing sports, reading novels, walking through the woods, conversing with friends are all activities, but not creative ones: they are not engaged in so as to bring something into being. Neither is carrying out some mechanical operation in a factory a form of 'creative' activity in Marx's sense. Although it is productive, it belongs to the realm of necessity rather than that of freedom: we need to remember that on the interpretation of Marx's theory that Elster provides, Marx is not arguing that *any* kind of work is a human need, only its autonomous variety.[1] But he needs an argument to show why a flourishing human life needs to encompass such creativeness. Why could it not be devoted wholly to activities in the non-creative category?

It would not do to argue that creative activity is activity for others – as outlined above – and that an individual's flourishing contains a necessary altruistic element. If both these things were true, then a life made up of *certain* non-creative activities – playing sports or reading novels, for instance, or any others in the above list – could well be too self-contained to qualify as flourishing. But this would still leave plenty of possible altruistic activities of a non-creative sort, from household chores to aspirin-production.

Suppose we left out the latter and concentrated only on activities like novel-reading and country walks, in which nothing is produced for others' benefit. Could a flourishing life consist only of these? The issue is whether a life of personal well-being must intentionally do something to benefit others – the issue in dispute between Thrasymachus and Socrates in Plato's *Republic*. I will not attempt to resolve it here, although we shall be returning to it later. The only point I wish to make is that, if this is indeed an issue for Marx, to make his case he needs to come down on the Socratic, altruistic side. (He also needs, as I have said, to exclude chores, etc from the reckoning.)

Arguments about individuals' flourishing often tend to get conflated in Marx with arguments about human flourishing in general. It would be hard to deny, as we have seen, that work in some form is necessary for any human society to prosper. This is most obviously true of work directed to meeting biological needs – for food, shelter, health, etc. It may also be possible to argue that creative work – by artists, scientists, philosophers, etc – is essential for the continued well-being of a certain kind of society, perhaps a liberal one. But even if both these claims are true, they do nothing to show that work of either sort need be a constituent of every individual's flourishing. We need to keep the two considerations firmly apart.

Putting all these various arguments from Marx together, we are driven to conclude that none of them shows that work – in some sense or other – *must* be a component, centrally or otherwise, in personal well-being. I turn now to three contemporary philosophers, all influenced by Marx, who seek to support the same conclusion.

Attfield

Robin Attfield (1984) follows Marx in making a connexion between work and the human essence. Specifically, his argument is about 'meaningful work'. This is roughly equivalent to what I have labelled 'autonomous work', implying that the worker values the product as of personal significance to him or her and also autonomously, both in applying skill or judgment and also in having some say in planning the work.

Meaningful work is found not only in paid employment, but also, for instance, in study at school or university, care of the young, the old, voluntary work for charities, housework and gardening (p 145). It also includes the production of theories and works of art (p 148). The link with the human essence comes in the statement – taken as an interpretation of a view presented by Marx – that 'an essential capacity of human beings is the capacity for meaningful work' (p 148).

As to what Attfield means by 'essential capacity' and its relevance to issues of flourishing, the following quotation from him provides the clue:

> Let the essential capacities of a species be those capacities in the absence of which from most members of the species it would not be the species which it is. In this sense, of course, what is essential need not be distinctive but may be common to several species, just as what is distinctive may be quite inessential. Now it is, I maintain, a necessary truth that to live well, develop, or flourish as a member of a species involves being able to exercise the essential capacities of the species. Thus to flourish as a jaguar requires command of many faculties common to mammals, plus others such as the ability to run faster than most others can. And similarly a human only lives well if he or she is able to exercise essential human capacities; and is benefited by being able to do so. (p 145)

According to Attfield, the capacity for meaningful work is as much an essential capacity of human beings as the capacity for linguistic communication. Although infants, senile and mentally defective people may not have this capacity, 'it is not a requirement for an essential capacity that all members of the species concerned should currently be able to exercise it. The question is rather whether a species of which not as many as most members possessed this capacity or potential would be human. ... most human beings do manifestly possess a capacity for meaningful work' (p 147).

In the further development of his position, Attfield states that 'it follows by the argument from essential capacities that the ability to exercise meaningful work is necessarily a benefit to people, and that they are harmed by the failure to come by it, the harm lying in their failure to develop as people' (p 148). From this he argues to the natural right that human beings possess to meaningful work. Since 'for most people the best hope for meaningful work lies in paid employment' (p 149), Attfield favours slowing down the introduction of microprocessors because this leads to unemployment. 'Rather than laying off workers and preventing school-leavers from finding opportunities to work, societies such as Britain ... should aim at full employment ...' (p 150).

Appearing as it does in the very first issue of *Applied Philosophy*, Attfield's essay is a bold attempt to generate policy conclusions via philosophical reasoning. But its basic premises, about essential capacities and their relation to well-being, raise difficulties.

Let us take as read Attfield's definition of essential capacities as those which have to be possessed by most members of a species for it to be the species it is. This is not unproblematic – especially in its quantifying approach (why 50+ per cent?) – but we can let that pass. The question on which to focus is in what sense is the capacity for meaningful work an essential one? It is no doubt true that most human beings, unlike crabs, trees or boulders, are not debarred by their constitution from being able to engage in it. Given appropriate circumstances, including relevant forms of learning and opportunities, most of us could undertake it. But this interpretation of Attfield's thesis does not get us very far. In exactly the same sense, most human beings – unlike crabs, trees or boulders – have the capacity to eat hamburgers or the capacity to read *The Sun*. Are these then also among our essential capacities?

All this raises difficulties for the next leg of the argument connecting essential capacities with flourishing. It is said to be 'a necessary truth that to live well, develop, or flourish as a member of a species involves being able to exercise the essential capacities of the species'. But *why* is this a necessary truth? It may be true that human beings cannot flourish without exercising their capacities to communicate linguistically; but it is hard to think how one could show that we must come to grief if we never watch *Blind Date* or play the National Lottery.

If this criticism is right, then Attfield's further claims, about a natural right to meaningful work and about the need for full employment, lack support and his attempt to revitalise Marx's link between work and the human essence founders. I leave out of account further problems in establishing these further claims, especially the conclusion that there should be a policy of full employment. If meaningful work is indeed autonomous work in my terms – and not simply work which offers opportunities for autonomous decision-making – one wonders how many jobs in the economy could provide this. How many people would choose as an ideal goal in their life – helping it to have great personal significance to them – making zip-fasteners, sending out gas bills or mending potholes?

One final word on Attfield. As with several of the philosophers whose views we shall now examine, his account seems attached to the work culture. Not that he would have any truck with the extreme position held by Mary Warnock (1977), for instance, that it is probably better to have *any* kind of job than no job at all (see above, p 2) – quite the contrary. But his advocacy of full employment seems to stamp him as a productivist. He certainly nowhere suggests that work within the economic system should lose its traditional centrality.

The need to work

I turn now to philosophers who see work (in some form) as a basic human need. Most of what I have to say is about the views of Richard Norman and Sean Sayers. But a brief word, first, about a third text in the same tradition, by Len Doyal and Ian Gough (1991).

Doyal and Gough claim that the human need to participate in the overall division of labour in one's society is derived from a more basic human need for personal autonomy.

As we shall see in more detail later on, human needs may be understood in more than one way – as what is necessary for human beings to survive, or as what is necessary for their well-being, given further specification of what is to count as well-being. Food and shelter are survival needs (as well as well-being needs). Parental love does not seem to be a survival need, but it may well be a well-being need in any human society. Personal liberty and income may be well-being needs in a modern liberal society, but not in some other human societies.

Since personal autonomy has virtually no part in the value-system of a tradition-directed society, Doyal and Gough's frame of reference seems to be well-being needs in a modern liberal-democratic society. There may be a problem in calling personal autonomy a 'need': it seems to be more a defining value of liberal democracy than a necessary condition of it – being unlike (negative) liberty in this respect. But even if it is a need, it does not seem to imply as a derivative need participation in the overall division of labour. One can flourish as an autonomous person, if one is rich enough, without participating in the division of labour at all. Whether or not this is desirable is another matter: the point is that participation does not seem to be necessary for one's flourishing and only if it is necessary can it properly be said to be a need.

Richard Norman

Richard Norman's argument for meaningful work as a basic need is part of a larger project in ethical naturalism which seeks to base ethical values in human nature. The 'needs' route is attractive from this point of view. It is through reflection on what we are like as human beings that we quickly light on our biological needs for food, water, air, shelter and so on whose satisfaction is so central to our flourishing. Norman extends this list of needs beyond the physical to such things as psychic harmony, sexual fulfilment, being treated as persons not objects, creativeness and rootedness (Norman, 1983, p 239). Included in the extended list is 'meaningful, unalienated work'. This term is not further defined. It may be close to Attfield's notion of meaningful work. Nothing turns on this as far as my discussion of Norman's position is concerned.

What is work of this kind necessary *for?* Norman makes a general distinction, applicable to the whole range of needs, between what is necessary for mental health, 'understood as that harmony of the personality which enables a person to function effectively' (p 240) and what is needed for a life of happiness and fulfilment. He further suggests 'that those needs which have to be satisfied in order for one to be able to function effectively are the same needs whose fuller satisfaction makes for a richly happy life' (p 241). In other words, where, a few paragraphs ago, I made a distinction of kind between biological needs and well-being needs, Norman is close to making this a difference of degree. I will not take up the issues this raises for the philosophy of needs in general, but concentrate on its bearing on the value of work.

As regards the first level of needs, that of effective functioning, Norman states that human beings, among other things, 'need to engage in activities which are not totally mindless and mechanical' (ibid.). He goes on to say that 'it is also the case that the richest enjoyments and satisfactions of human life are to be found the further meeting of these same needs – in work which uses to the full one's creative capacities, and in the life of the emotions, and the many different kinds of human love and solidarity' (ibid.).

It might well be true that if people engaged in no other activities than mindless and mechanical ones their mental health would suffer. But even if one accepts that well-being needs are different in degree rather than in kind, it does not follow that work of some sort is a well-being need: it merely follows that activity which uses one's intelligence to a high degree is such a need. The point here is that there are many kinds of intelligent activities and only some of them have to do with producing things. Enjoying rather than creating works of art; playing games; witty conversation – these and other things can be undertaken with great finesse and judgment, but none of them need be undertaken as work. If work is indeed a human need,it must itself be necessary for some further end, e.g. personal well-being, and not merely a member of a class of things (e.g. highly intelligent activities) which is necessary for it.

I conclude that Norman has not made out a valid case here for meaningful work as a human need, whatever interpretation one gives to 'meaningful'.

Elsewhere in his book, in the course of a discussion of Marx's ethical views on work, he produces further arguments 'for the claim that work is so important for self-realisation' (p 177).

There is, first, the sheer quantitative dominance of work in relation to other activities. The work which people do to maintain themselves and their dependants engages a great deal of their time, and because it bulks so large it does more than anything else to shape the general character of their lives. Then there is its inescapability. Other activities which people perform are largely a matter of individual choice, but work is the one activity which almost all human beings (other than the young, the old, or the excessively privileged) have to perform in order to maintain themselves. For this reason it forms the common core of people's lives, which sets the pattern for their general character. Finally, there is the fact that people's work is the most clearly public aspect of their lives. It is their work above all that defines them in the eyes of others – and I have stressed previously the importance of being recognised by others as an aspect of self-realisation. Putting all of this together, we can say that what you are is primarily a matter of what you do, and what you do is primarily a matter of what work you perform (pp 177–178).

This passage lucidly shows the central place that work has – as a matter of fact – in our lives. If it is not only an empirical fact but also a good thing that work should be so central, one could then go on to ask which kinds of work are desirable and which undesirable and it is not difficult to see how one might make out a case for meaningful rather than mindless work. But how does one get from the empirical fact to the positive value judgment? If work is indeed so quantitatively dominant over other activities in our lives, that is not necessarily to be welcomed, as we have seen ourselves in the earlier critique of the centrality of work in our culture. It might be something we should have less of.

Norman comes near this point in his answer to the objection

that the reasons just given for making work so central are, in fact, historically transitory. It may be argued that with increasing automation the production of material necessities requires less and less labour time, and that there is a real prospect that in the future people may need to devote only a small portion of their time to work (p 178)

He is inclined to think that even if the average working day were halved (in his eyes a utopian idea) 'work would still play a large part in people's organisation of their time' (ibid.), although he gives no reasons in support.

He is also inclined to think that there may be truth in the objection that 'work has been given its present quantitative and qualitative importance only in modern industrial societies' (ibid.), concluding from this that perhaps

the need for self-realisation through work is indeed historically and culturally specific. Even so it can still be maintained, at the very least, that within our own society the need is a real and objective one. The idea that one's work determines one's identity, and the stimulus to invest one's energies in that work, are so deeply embedded in our culture that no one could now find full satisfaction in a life which did not contain its component of meaningful work. (p 179)

This final position seems to me decidedly shaky. In fact, we have been here before – a couple of paragraphs ago. The centrality of work is certainly deeply embedded in the culture. But this fact does nothing to shore up the evaluative conclusion that in our society work is a well-being (or self-realisation) need. For all we know, people's well-being in that society may be best served by challenging and undermining work's hegemony. We may, for all we know, do well to reject the view that work determines our identity: perhaps we would flourish better if attachment to work were not so indelibly a part of us.

Sean Sayers

Sean Sayers (1988) defends the central contention in Marxist socialism 'that socially productive labour is, in Marx's words, man's essential activity' (p 722). Like Norman, whose views are also in the Marxist tradition, if less tied to Marx's writings themselves, Sayers believes there is a human need to work. 'Work' he defines as a form of productive activity directed towards useful ends. It is also for the most part a social activity (pp 726–727). He seems ambivalent on whether or not 'work' should be equated with 'a job', with 'paid employment'. On the one hand, he states that there are many kinds of work which do not take the form of a job, not least domestic work traditionally performed by women (p 727). On the other hand, we find statements like 'women feel a *need* – an inner need – for work: a need for a job as an end in itself ...' (p 728); or 'the socialist principle of the "right to work" is a demand for jobs' (p 729).

Leaving this last discrepancy on one side, we can see that Sayers' definition is narrower than the one I proposed in Chapter 1. He wants to restrict 'work' to activity aimed at useful ends, whereas I treated it only as activity directed towards some kind of end-product, not necessarily a useful one. If something is useful, it is a means to some end. But, following my account, producing a work of art counts as work even though one's symphony or poem is created as an object of intrinsic interest. There might also be 'useless work' in another sense – as in our earlier example of soldiers kept busy by cutting grass with scissors (p 9 above). As suggested then, this might be seen as valuable obedience-training. But even if it falls as a counterexample to the claim that work is necessarily directed towards useful ends, the art example still stands. In any case, it is not at all clear that Sayers would agree that the soldiers' activity has a useful end product: 'useful', for him, is to be understood as 'useful for the satisfaction of human needs' (see p 727) and I do not know whether he would see the military end in question as falling under this.

How does Sayers support his claim that there is a human need to work? He distances himself from the view, which he locates in Norman, that this is rooted in the unique creativity to be found in human nature 'which distinguishes us from the rest of animal creation' (p 732). The socialist view of work 'rejects the idea of a universal and eternal human nature'. Human nature changes historically. 'Through the activity of labour, people develop their powers and capacities and create new needs – including the need to work'. This has not always been so. In hunter-gatherer societies, indeed in many other pre-industrial societies, this need had not yet developed. Industrialism has brought with it a new emphasis on work and the virtues of work:

> Thus the modern need to work, although it is undoubtedly a historically developed need, should not be judged 'false' or 'artificial' simply for that reason. On the contrary, it is a real and ineliminable feature of contemporary psychology. For in the course of the historical developments I have been outlining, new habits, new attitudes, new needs have been created and old ones relinquished. Human nature itself has been transformed. (p 736)

My difficulty with this argument is the same as that I have with Norman's. Facts about the emphasis industrial societies have placed on work or about individuals' attachment to the work ethic are one thing, the contention that we have a need to work, another. One simply cannot derive the latter from the former.

So we are still left wondering why Sayers insists on this need. What does he see work as necessary for? He does not go into this, so we can only speculate. Is it necessary to individual flourishing? Perhaps as a Marxist he would reject the 'individualism' embedded in this notion. Is it necessary (in contemporary industrial societies) not to individuals but to humanity as such as part of its historical development? I do not know whether Sayers would want to say this. If he did, we would have to tackle the credentials of Marxist theory as a whole, which is beyond my present remit.

Although it is not surprising that a Marxist writer like Sayers should wish solidly to defend the alleged human need to work, given the centrality which Marx attached to productive work as 'the first premise of all human existence' (Marx and Engels 1965, p 48), it is disappointing at the same time that he sees so little virtue in the idea – also found in Marx, as we have seen – of liberating people, at least to some degree, from work's constraints, especially the time it takes up in and dominance over people's lives. For him, socialism demands 'not the liberation of people from work ... but rather the liberation of work ... from the stultifying confines of the capitalist system (p 740)'. I do not see why there need be an 'either-or'. If personal autonomy is an important value, some kind of diminution of the power of the work ethic over our lives would seem reasonable – but here, perhaps, the cast of mind of Marxist socialism is at odds with that of a more liberal-democratic version. As will become clear, if it is insufficiently clear already, my own alignment is with the latter.

THE RIGHT TO MEANINGFUL WORK

The case for work, or meaningful work, as a human need has not been sub-stantiated. Other philosophers have argued for what might also be called mean-ingful work, but on different grounds. I examine now the views of Simone Weil and Adina Schwartz.

Simone Weil

Simone Weil interrupted her career as a lycée teacher from 1934–1935 to work as an unskilled labourer in various factories around Paris. She paints a vivid picture of the wearisomeness, monotony and above all inhumanity of the work in her essay 'Factory Work'. Yet despite her revulsion, she does not do what many others do and look outside the factory for human fulfilment. To antici-pate later discussion, she does not, like Hannah Arendt and her followers, exalt what Arendt calls 'work', i.e. the autonomous making of enduring products, over 'labour'. Neither does she, like André Gorz (1985), see human flourishing as a function of the liberation from paid employment produced by a radical reduction in working hours. In her view

> All systems of social reform or transformation seem to miss the point. Were they to be realised, the evil would be left intact. … Some promise a ridicu-lously exaggerated reduction of the work-day. But the conversion of a people into a swarm of idlers, who for two hours a day would be slaves, is neither desirable nor morally possible, if materially so. No one would accept two daily hours of slavery … If there is a remedy, it is of a different order, less easily conceivable … It is necessary to transform incentives, to reduce or abolish the relation of worker to factory, of worker to machine, and to make possible a radically changed awareness of the passing of time while working. (p 66)

For Weil, it is not long hours at factory work which are the problem, but the servile conditions in which people have to work. There is no hint of doubt about the centrality of work, even work like this, to human existence. The way ahead, once what can be automated has been automated, lies in such things as relieving workers from the tyranny of isolated processes by giving them an understanding of the whole operation and what social ends it serves:

> The case would be different if a workingman knew clearly, from day to day, moment to moment, just what part he was playing in every step of the pro-ductive process and what place the factory occupied in society. If a work-ingman's job is to drop a die-punch on a piece of brass designed for some device on the subway line, he ought to know it. (p 70)

Time and rhythm are close to Weil's heart. Workers should be allowed to work more self-directedly at their own pace and to relate what they do to mean-ingful future objectives rather than being prisoners of the present.

The solution of the problem implies not only a certain knowledge on the part of each worker of the functioning of the factory as a whole, but an organisation of the factory that makes for some kind of autonomy of each shop unit in relation to the whole establishment, of each worker in relation to his shop ... Each workingman ought to know more or less what will be expected of him a week or a fortnight in advance (ibid.)

While it is fairly obvious how these various changes would be to the advantage of the factory worker, it is harder to understand why Weil appears to set no store by reducing working hours. Two hours' drudgery a day seems patently better than eight or nine. Despite what she says, I think many people *would* accept two hours' 'slavery' every day if it left them with the other twenty-two to do what they wanted. Of course, this would not be as good as two hours of more congenial work, perhaps on the lines of Weil's reforms; but it would equally be nowhere near as bad as four times more 'slavery'. Weil also believes that liberated factory workers would become a 'swarm of idlers'. But why assume this rather than that this would give them more time for their own projects?

More light is shed on Weil's position in the following passage

Time and rhythm constitute the most important factor of the whole problem of work. Certainly it is not the work itself that is at issue. It is at once inevitable and fitting that work should involve monotony and tedium; indeed, what considerable earthly undertakings in whatever domain have ever been free of tedium and monotony? There is more monotony in a Gregorian Chant or a Bach Concerto than in an operetta. This world into which we are cast does exist; we are truly flesh and blood; we have been thrown out of eternity; and we are indeed obliged to journey painfully through time, minute in and minute out. This travail is our lot and the monotony of work is but one of the forms which it assumes (p 69)

She goes on to say that it is the *kind* of monotony – the 'identity of the moments, which succeed one another like the ticking of a clock' – not monotony itself, which is amiss. Workers, as we saw above, need to be able to relate what they do to what comes later. 'The future must be opened up for the workingman through removal of the blinders that keep him from exercising his sense of foresight' (p 70).

Weil's views on the value of monotony in human life are counterintuitive. The argument seems weak. Take the sentence: 'It is at once inevitable and fitting that work should involve monotony and tedium; indeed, what considerable earthly undertakings in whatever domain have ever been free of tedium and monotony?' The thought seems to be that since work is a 'considerable earthly undertaking', like Bach's music and other such undertakings it is fitting that it be monotonous. There are two points to make here. The value of whatever monotony there is in music is aesthetic, whether to do with formal properties, like the contrast of the ground bass with the melody, or expressive, like the repeated patterns in a Beethoven symphony. There seems no parallel with the monotony of factory work. This has not been deliberately created as an aesthetic object; monotony has not been crafted into it as a way of heightening an aesthetic effect. When assessing the positive or negative value of monotony in *this* context, it is not aesthetic, but ethical, values that we have in mind. Prima facie, monotony is a *dis*value, because people find it distressing. It is logically adrift to try to override this presumption by switching from ethical to aesthetic value.

The second point is the apparent assumption that work is a 'considerable earthly undertaking'. What does Simone Weil have in mind? No doubt the answer lies in the second part of the quotation, in her picture of human life as a painful journey, as 'travail'. We are clearly in the presence of a traditional Christian conception, of fallen human beings' life as a struggle through a vale of tears. One can begin to see how monotonous work, as one form of suffering, can play an exalted role, how the nobility of enduring it – as Simone Weil herself willingly endured it – can elevate it to the highest rank of human achievements, equatable with Gregorian Chant and worthier than operetta.

It is less puzzling, given all this, that Weil should attach negative weight to reducing working hours. To do so would strike at the heart of the Christian's understanding of human nature. It would remove from our path the rocks and thorns which make it so painful. Toil would be no longer at the spiritual centre of our existence.

How far one follows Weil depends partly on how far one shares her religious starting-point. I have to reject what she says because I do not.

Adina Schwartz

Adina Schwartz (1982) also writes about routine factory work. Her starting point is different from Simone Weil's – liberal-democratic rather than Christian – but her criticism of present arrangements, together with the changes she recommends, overlaps to some extent.

> Individual workers do not decide how to perform their particular jobs. Instead of being hired to achieve certain goals and left to select and pursue adequate means, workers are employed to perform precisely specified actions. Even the order in which they perform those operations, the pace at which they work, and the particular bodily movements they employ are largely determined by others' decisions. (p 634)

Schwartz begins from 'the widely held view that a just society respects all its members as autonomous agents' (p 635). Since mechanical work is incompatible with personal autonomy, it follows that 'we must demand that no one be employed at the sorts of jobs that have just been described' (ibid.): government action is necessary 'so that all persons' jobs foster instead of stunt their autonomous development' (p 646).

To the objection that 'an individual's work is not his or her whole life' (p 636) and that he or she could be self-directed in their non-working life, Schwartz replies that this is problematic on both empirical and a priori grounds. Psychologists have shown that

> when persons work for considerable lengths of time at jobs that involve mainly mechanical activity, they tend to be made less capable of and less interested in rationally framing, pursuing, and adjusting their own plans during the rest of the time. (p 637)

This conclusion is also supported, philosophically, by the thought that becoming autonomous is a 'process of integrating one's personality, of seeing all one's pursuits as subject to one's activity of planning and to view all one's experiences as providing a basis for evaluating and adjusting one's beliefs, methods and aims' (p 638): the radical division of a life into autonomous and non-autonomous domains 'fosters schizophrenia' (ibid.).

Finally, Schwartz rejects two common suggestions for dealing with mechanical work since they do not meet the requirements of autonomy. Job-enlargement by rotating jobs still leaves work precisely specified; and worker participation in democratic decision-making still leaves relations between managers and detail workers hierarchical (pp 640–641). The only solution is that 'tasks must be shared out in a way that abolishes the distinction between those who decide and those who execute others' decisions' (p 641); there must be a 'democratic division of labour that will ensure that no one is employed mainly at routine operations' (p 644).

Richard Arneson (1987) disagrees with Schwartz's implied conclusion that everyone in paid employment in an advanced industrial society should be engaged in, and have the right to be engaged in, meaningful work, that is, work which is interesting, calls for intelligence and initiative, gives the worker considerable freedom over procedures and a genuinely democratic say over the work process and overall policies. His central objection is that this would be paternalistic on the part of the state, since it would be privileging one kind of option (meaningful work) for the autonomous chooser over others. Not everyone would want 'intensive and lengthy policy-making discussions' (p 536). In the market socialist society which Arneson favours it is conceivable that 'job qualifications will be set so that some persons have no options other than rote, boring, meaningless work' (ibid.). The crucial requirement is 'that anyone who must take dirty work is compensated for it so that her life prospects are roughly as advantageous overall as the life prospects of the more talented' (ibid.). In addition, some people who have the talent to qualify for more challenging jobs may still prefer a non-stimulating job if it brings with it compensating advantages.

Arneson deals with Schwartz's psychological objection that mechanical work unfits people for autonomous activity in the rest of their lives by claiming that this at most gives a reason for governments to provide information to intending workers about this risk. Beyond that, it is up to individuals to decide how to weight deterioration in rational faculties against whatever positive advantages they see in non-meaningful work.

Arneson's anti-paternalist critique of Schwartz is particularly telling because it rests on the same value – personal autonomy – as Schwartz's own paper. He is apparently less moved than Schwartz – and indeed Weil – by the affront to human dignity which both other writers see in mechanical work – not moved sufficiently, that is, to call for its elimination. He appears to have no objection to people doing this for eight hours a day throughout their working lives, as long as this is what they rationally choose for whatever reason.

At this point I find myself somewhere in between Arneson and Schwartz. The latter writes about people working 'for considerable lengths of time at jobs that involve mainly mechanical activity'. Her whole argument assumes the usual pattern of full-time employment. This complicates her case, especially her denial that detail workers could be autonomous in their non-work time. Her reliance on the psychological argument about mental deterioration only makes sense if workers are working something like a full day every day. If they were to do only one or two hours a day, the psychological argument would be very weak. So would the *a priori* argument, that autonomy requires mental integration and this would be impossible with non-meaningful work. We do not see people as on the edge of schizophrenia if they spend an hour or so a day washing up and doing other mechanical household chores. An hour or so in a factory is unlikely to tip them over it.

All this raises the question whether what disturbs Schwartz is mechanical work as such, or mechanical work in conventional conditions of something like a forty hour week. Her case is strong against the latter, weak against the former. I agree with Arneson that she has not shown that mechanical work as such should be outlawed. There may be people willing to take it on for short stints, especially if it gave them plenty of scope to pursue their autonomous interests outside the job.

Has Schwartz shown that mechanical work on a full-time, long-term basis should be outlawed? Let us suppose that it would indeed tend to produce some deterioration of one's rational faculties. Could it be something that an autonomous person could rationally choose? Arneson would, as far as I can see, answer 'yes', given that the rewards were great enough and given that choice was fully informed and uncoerced. In addition, as we have seen, he thinks it possible in his socialist polity that some persons – i.e. those unqualified for other things – 'have no options other than rote, boring, meaningless work'. My own view is that given that, generally speaking, virtually no one would choose such work on a long-term basis, both because of its unpleasantness and because of its effects on mental functioning, assuming they knew them, there would seem to be a case for outlawing *long hours* in such employment, where these were necessary in order to gain a living wage. This would presumably suit Arneson's poorly qualified group. It is hard to imagine who might fall into his other category – people who could do meaningful work but would autonomously choose meaningless work on a long-term basis. But if there were such people, the legislation in question might be framed to suit them, too. If they wanted to work mechanically over the statutory maximum of ten or twenty hours a week, some kind of enabling clause might permit this. (On the other hand, would there be much point in building in clauses to accommodate virtually no one except the occasional masochist? Even without them, the masochist could always try to find ways of breaking the law.)

It is interesting that neither Schwartz nor Arneson puts the spotlight on the extent of heteronomous work and its centrality in our culture. Schwartz touches on this implicitly, as we have seen, but takes as her target mechanical work as such, not its domination of people's lives. Arneson does not even touch on it.

A last point on Adina Schwartz. The core value in her paper is personal autonomy. She is looking for a way of organising paid employment so that it promotes rather than hinders autonomy. She wants industrial employment to be 'arranged so that all persons' jobs allow them to act as autonomous individuals' (p 642). Her solution, as we have seen, is to share work out in a way that abolishes the distinction between managers and managed and makes sure that no one spends their time mainly on routine operations.

My query is whether workers in these idealised conditions would indeed necessarily be acting as autonomous individuals. They would certainly be involved in democratic decision-making within the firm and this would give them more options than monotonous routine work. But is this enough for autonomy? Sometimes workers in actual companies belong to 'quality circles', or groups with similar titles, who are responsible for allocating work among themselves. If this happened wholly at the level of routine work, Schwartz would presumably object that this contravened the autonomy principle. The major goals of the enterprise would still be determined elsewhere, the workers in question being able to decide only on procedures. In Schwartz's ideal, every worker participates in setting the major goals. But this could well be at odds with his or her autonomy. For autonomy is *personal* autonomy. It has to do with how people organise their lives, or, in Schwartz's words, with 'rationally form(ing) and act(ing) on some overall conception of what they want in life' (p 635). How far a person's major life-goals coincide with the major goals of an industrial firm is quite another matter. Imagine an ideal Schwartzian factory that is making supermarket trolleys. Even though employees are able collectively to make major policy decisions, it does not follow that for each of them manufacturing supermarket trolleys is a major personal goal, one of the things that they most want to get out of life. (This goes back to the distinctions made earlier between *autonomous work* and *autonomy in work*). If any of them does have such a life ambition, then he or she will be engaged in autonomous work. But this is highly unlikely. People typically have major goals like success in the eyes of the world, a happy home life, friendship, respect, personal projects of an intellectual, artistic or practical sort, and so on. I have never heard of anyone who would put manufacturing supermarket trolleys on a par with things like these and cannot imagine what such an individual would be like. Much more plausibly, a person might be willing to participate in company goals to do with making trolleys, despite their personal lack of significance to them, so that he or she might better realise some of their own goals. Their work would be heteronomous. How far it could still be the work of an autonomous person, even though not itself a form of autonomous work, would depend on whether helping to realise company goals was chosen as a rational way of trying to further personal goals. But it is just at this point that internal decision-making within the firm, the decision-making that Schwartz thinks so crucial for workers to be autonomous agents, drops out of the picture. If what is important for personal autonomy is that one correctly sees what one does in the firm as a good means to realising one's major goals, then earning sky-high wages for routine work might for many people be a better bet than taking part in democratic decision-making. There is no direct route from personal autonomy to autonomy as a worker: the former value does not imply the latter. Neither does the latter imply the former: whether in a quality circle or in some radically more democratic system, the major goals of the institution may have precious little connexion with one's major personal goals.

WORK AND LABOUR

Hannah Arendt is well-known for the distinction she makes in *The Human Condition* (1958) between 'labour' and 'work':

> Labor is the activity which corresponds to the biological process of the human body, whose spontaneous growth, metabolism, and eventual decay are bound to the vital necessities produced and fed into the life process by labor. ... Work is the activity which corresponds to the unnaturalness of human existence, which is not imbedded in, and whose mortality is not compensated by, the species' ever-recurring life cycle. Work provides an 'artificial' world of things, distinctly different from all natural surroundings. Within its borders each individual life is housed, while this world itself is meant to outlast and transcend them all. (p 9)

Arendt's distinction is not wholly clear from this passage, but from her further elaborations it is evident that labour has to do with producing what is necessary for human beings to live, its products – food, clothing etc – being immediately consumed and replaced in an endless cycle. The products of work, on the other hand, are permanent objects intended mostly for use and to last over generations.

Arendt's distinction has been picked up by a number of writers who urge that work should replace labour, either in some specific sphere or more generally. Writing about university education, P Herbst (1973) says:

> The central idea of this paper is to apply a distinction of Hannah Arendt's

to the educational scene; the distinction between work and labour. The thesis is briefly that education is work rather than labour, and that to educate well is to work, as well as to teach people to work. (p 59)

P D Anthony (1977) discusses 'the ideology of work' in general, criticising the different arguments across the centuries, but especially in our times, by which slave-owners, religious bodies, socialists and capitalists have buttressed the belief that hard work is a vital ingredient of human life. He writes:

> Labouring may be part of an elemental cycle but it is work, the making of things for use, that appears to be the more satisfying activity. (p 278)

and also

> If work has become purposeless it is because, although it is necessary, the imminent connexion between work and survival has become obscure, at least in complex industrial societies. But if that is so, purpose may be restored by turning (in the terms used by Hannah Arendt) from labour to work, to making things. (p 315)

Although Herbst, Anthony and others make ethical recommendations of this sort, it is not too clear to me how far Arendt herself would also want to do this. 'Labour' and 'work' are indeed prominent categories in her overall argument, but they have their place within a grander theme. A third category at the same logical level is 'action'. This is 'the only activity that goes on directly between men without the intermediary of things or matter' (Arendt 1958, p 9) and is concerned with human relationships, not least at the political level. 'Labour', 'work' and 'action' are the three constituents of the '*vita activa*', itself to be distinguished from the '*vita contemplativa*'. The topic of Arendt's book is major shifts of priority within the *vita activa* and between the latter and the *vita contemplativa* in Western history since the Greeks. The thrust is historical and analytical rather than ethical. 'My contention is simply that the enormous weight of contemplation in the traditional hierarchy has blurred the distinctions and articulations within the *vita activa* itself' (p 17). Again, 'my use of the term *vita activa* presupposes that the concern underlying all its activities is not the same as and is neither superior nor inferior to the central concern of the *vita contemplativa* ' (pp 17–18).

We must avoid getting drawn too far into Arendt's larger themes, most of which are irrelevant to our purposes. Work and labour come into her historical thesis as follows. While at times, among Greek thinkers for example, political life (as a form of 'action') has been the dominant value within the *vita activa*, at other times work and labour have been supreme. With the 'reversal of the hierarchical order between the *vita contemplativa* and the *vita activa*' (p 262) in favour of the latter during the seventeenth century, work acquired a new salience. 'First among the activities within the *vita activa* to rise to the position formerly occupied by contemplation were the activities of making and fabricating – the prerogatives of *homo faber*' (p 268). Arendt points to the 'instrumentalisation of the world' which grew up in the early modern age, *homo faber*'s 'confidence in tools and in the productivity of the maker of artificial objects, his trust in the all-comprehensive range of the means-end category' (p 279). Very quickly, however, there was a further reversal of priorities within the *vita activa* with the elevation of labouring (p 280). The rise of industrialism, Marxism and the consumer society all meant 'the victory of the *Animal Laborans*' (p 292), the work of *homo faber* being increasingly restricted to that of the artist (p 296).

Like her mentor Heidegger's *Being and Time* (Heidegger 1962), Arendt's book is intended not as a work of ethics but as an examination of what is the case. Both works are in a sense descriptions of the human condition. At the same time, just as in Heidegger, Arendt's ethical values are visible at times through the text. This is especially so in disparaging references to the dominance of labour in the closing pages of the book – to the 'loss of human experience' (p 294) which this has brought about, or to the thought that 'the modern age – which began with such an unprecedented and promising outburst of human activity – may end in the deadliest, most sterile passivity history has ever known' (p 295). Arendt's strictures are not directed against labour itself. She is not advocating that labour should be replaced by something else. To do so would be odd indeed: for one thing, the human race would soon die out, as no one would produce any food. Paralleling to some extent this present essay, her book regrets the centrality of labour in modern conceptions of human life. While what she is against is reasonably clear, it is less obvious what she is for. Quite possibly she does not intend us to know this. Whether labour's pre-eminence in the *vita activa* should pass to the fabrication of enduring objects or to civic involvement is not spelt out. Neither is the balance to be struck between the *vita activa* and the *vita contemplativa*.

Unlike some of her followers, Arendt is not advocating that labour should be replaced by work. This is not in itself to imply that such advocates are misguided, since distinctions, once made, can be put to purposes beyond their maker's. All the same, they may be misguided. As we have just seen, the elimination of labour means the elimination of the human race. This aside, it may not do to lean too heavily on Arendt's distinction between 'labour' and 'work', partly because it may not bear much weight, but also because it may lack comprehensiveness.

Clear-cut cases of 'labour' would be tilling fields to grow corn or tending a spinning machine in a cotton mill. Here one is using one's body to help produce the eternally replaceable necessities of life. But what if one is a manager in a clothing or food factory? Does that, too, count as 'labour' even though one is using one's brain rather than one's limbs and muscles?

Discussing the distinction between manual and intellectual work, Arendt seems almost in the same breath to include the latter as labour and then to exclude it:

The underlying tie between the laborer of the hand and the laborer of the head is again in the laboring process, in one case performed by the head, in the other by some other part of the body. Thinking, however, which is presumably the activity of the head, though it is in some ways like laboring – also a process which probably comes to an end only with life itself – is even less 'productive' than labor; if labor leaves no permanent trace, thinking leaves nothing tangible at all. (p 79)

Again, what if one is assembling parts of television sets or word processors? In what way is this 'activity which corresponds to the biological process of the human body'?

It would seem that Arendt shifts between different criteria in her account of 'labour'. Sometimes the emphasis is on producing life's necessities; sometimes on physical work; sometimes on producing consumer goods; sometimes on working to earn a living. In her most ample framework, virtually everybody is a labourer, teachers and judges as much as plumbers and waitresses: 'the artist ... strictly speaking, is the only 'worker' left in a laboring society' (p 111).

Similar, if less perplexing, problems arise with 'work'. Again, there is a clear enough paradigm: the craftsman, who produces some object – a grandfather clock, a carriage – intended for lasting use. *Homo faber,* Arendt tells us, 'relies entirely on the primordial tools of his hands' (p 126). Artists, as we have seen, are workers rather than labourers. Their products are outstandingly permanent (p147); even a poem is a tangible thing (p 149). Not only artists, but scholars, too, fall under the heading: Arendt speaks of men needing the help of *'homo faber* in his highest capacity, that is, the help of the artist. of poets and historiographers, of monument-builders or writers' (p 153). One source of difficulty here is how far the skilful manual use of tools is criterial. It fits the cabinet-maker; but not the historian – or even the poet. Cutting across this criterion is another, to do with the making of a lasting object. From this angle a philosophical or mathematical theory could be produced by 'work'. But then questions arise about the Royal Society, or the newly founded kingdom of Belgium in the nineteenth century, or even the National Lottery. Did creating these institutions count as 'work'?

The problem with Arendt's duo is their elasticity. It is not very clear what is included or excluded. Are they intended to be exhaustive of all kinds of work in the ordinary sense of the term? Would being a run-of-the-mill politician fit under one or the other category, or would it fall outside both? What about being a clergyman or a barrister?

Despite its celebrity, I am afraid I have not found Arendt's distinction particularly useful in examining work and its place in our lives. Her main contribution seems to reside, rather, in her critical stance to the centrality of largely heteronomous work in modern culture.

CHALLENGING CENTRALITY

Chapter 1 reminded us how deeply the assumption that (heteronomous) work should have a central, extensive place in human life has been embedded in British culture as well as in the modern world more generally. The shadows of the Puritan work-ethic are cast on our secular age, affecting the way individuals think of their lives, employment policy, the shape of the educational system.

But is the assumption defensible? It made sense within the religious framework of beliefs in which it was born in the sixteenth and seventeenth centuries. If we pull away this support, will it still stand up?

A striking feature of most of the philosophical writings on work just reviewed is their lack of interest in challenging the centrality assumption. The only exception is Hannah Arendt. Others' attention is elsewhere: on worker-participation, the right to meaningful work, defending work as a human need. When they do comment on work-reduction or liberation from work, as with Weil, Norman and Sayers for instance, their stance ranges from the ultra-cautious to the dismissive. All this is surprising viewed from a liberal vantage-point, since this work which is so dominant – and which is almost all heteronomous – puts so many constraints on people leading the sort of life they want. It seems so patently at odds with the ideal of autonomous well-being that one cannot imagine how radical thinkers could support it.

The answer is that not all radical thinkers about work are unalloyed liberals. Weil is in the Christian tradition, Norman to some extent and especially Sayers in the Marxist. As we have seen, both of these traditions have their own reasons for placing work centre-stage. They join hands in this with some economists, management theorists and other practitioners and ideologists of capitalism, although once again the supporting reasons are different. Some, but only some, of the latter tend to see workers primarily as instruments of production who need to work long stints to keep output and profits high. They in their turn, the crudest and most utilitarian of them, echo in modern terms the tenets of serf-owners and slave-owners throughout the ages.

Few philosophers have radically challenged this cross-ideological consensus on the centrality of work. Among the most notable have been Friedrich Nietzsche and Bertrand Russell. In *The Gay Science* Nietzsche is uncompromising:

> Virtues (like industriousness, obedience, chastity, filial piety, and justice) are usually harmful for those who possess them ... One praises the industrious even though they harm their eyesight or the spontaneity and freshness of their spirit. One honours and feels sorry for the youth who has worked himself into the ground because one thinks: 'For society as a whole the loss of even the best individual is merely a small sacrifice. Too bad that such sacrifices are needed! But it would be far worse if the individual would think otherwise and considered his preservation and development more important than his work in the service of society.' Thus one feels sorry for the youth not for his own sake but because a devoted instrument, ruthless

against itself – a so-called 'good man' – has been lost to society by his death. … Blindly raging industriousness … is represented as the way to wealth and honour … but one keeps silent about its dangers, its extreme dangerousness. That is how education always proceeds: one tries to condition an individual by various attractions and advantages to adopt a way of thinking and behaving that, once it has become a habit, instinct, passion, will dominate him to his own ultimate disadvantage but for the general good. (Nietzsche, 1974, Section 21)

Russell's (1932) essay 'In praise of idleness' (in Russell 1960) is equally scathing, equally critical of moral pressures to be diligent. He sees the origins of the modern cult of work in a pre-industrial serf/slave economy where it was in the interests of the élite to have others labouring for them and to believe that it was their duty to do so: 'The conception of duty, speaking historically, has been a means used by the holders of power to induce others to live for the interests of their masters rather than their own' (p12). He writes of the horror of the rich that the poor should have leisure, claiming, as against them, that the total pattern of work in our society could be reorganised so that for everyone it became restricted to four hours a day.

A contemporary eulogist of idleness is Philippe van Parijs (1995). The Californian surfer on the cover of his book does not want a job, preferring to spend his time in, or more accurately, on the water. This is his major goal as an autonomous person. Van Parijs argues in his book for a high basic income for everyone, regardless of whether they are in work or not. He suggests ways in which this basic income can be raised, e.g. by taxing job-holders.

Predictably, his ideas have not been universally popular among socialist philosophers. In a review of van Parijs' book, Ian Gough (1996, pp 82–83) writes:

Cooperative labour, including unpaid care work, is a defining feature of all social groups above a certain minimum size. The principle that all able-bodied persons should be enabled to contribute, and should actually then contribute, to the common wealth is a powerful component about intuitions about justice. 'Work' is not simply the antonym to 'leisure' and Van Parijs' liberal neutrality between the two is not morally convincing. Participation in universally socially significant activities, including work, is a crucial contributor to autonomy and human welfare. All able-bodied people should have the right – and the duty – to contribute to these productive activities.

Does Gough's argument against the surfer succeed? It may well be true that cooperative labour contributes to human welfare, but it does not follow from this that *all* able-bodied people have a duty to engage in it. In a society where all necessary work could be done by 75 per cent of able-bodied people, and where these autonomously chose to do this in preference to other things, why should the other 25 per cent who preferred not to work be morally bound to do so? Insisting on this would disadvantage them vis-à-vis the majority who were able to follow their preferences.

As I have been working on this essay, it has come to seem to me more and more extraordinary that we have taken the centrality assumption so much for granted in our culture. It seems to be so baseless that one wonders at how little – until recently – it has been challenged – except by those on the policy sidelines like Bertrand Russell, P D Anthony or André Gorz. But, as I come to think about it, I could say the same about other framework beliefs of the culture: belief in the existence of God, for instance. A hundred years ago this was commonly assumed, and the assumption was built into educational arrangements and other parts of the political system. Even today this is at least vestigially the case. Here, too, we have a taken-for-granted belief which seems to rest on nothing. Something of the same might be true of the traditional concept of British national character – as freedom-loving, Protestant, superior to Catholics and other less fortunate peoples and races, standing ever-ready to fight the enemy beyond the seas who threatens our religious and moral values. A lot of this is mythical and/or repulsive, yet well into this century it has been a cornerstone in many people's belief-systems, emerging rather more than vestigially in reactions to the Falklands crisis of 1982.

Bernard Williams (1985) has recently drawn our attention to another of these unfounded, framework beliefs. It is closely connected both with the belief in God and with traditional views of British national identity, but it also goes deep into the thought-worlds of many who reject them. This is the belief in the centrality of the notion of 'moral obligation' to our ethical life. In thinking how we should live, many of us, not only Christians, but also secular Kantians, utilitarians and others, see this first and foremost as a question of what we morally ought to do, of where our moral duty lies. Obligations of different sorts – to be honest, for instance, or to keep our promises, work for the common good or the general happiness, support our friends, care for our family, help those in misfortune, be benevolent and fair, develop our talents – are the main pillars of our lives. There may well be room in them for other things – for periods of relaxation or other kinds of pleasure, perhaps; but these are subsidiary, relatively insignificant graftings on to the main stem. Williams argues there is no good reason why the notion of moral obligation should dominate the ethical landscape to this extent. Obligations are an important feature of it, to be sure. If we make a promise or contract we are under an obligation to keep it. But there are other important ingredients, too, like personal well-being and virtues of character. For Williams, morality is a 'peculiar institution'. He means by this the traditional notion of morality rooted in the centrality of obligation. As I suspect has happened with other readers of his book, when I encountered his thesis I recognised the phenomenon about which he was writing both as something deeply present in my own outlook and, at the same time, as something quite groundless.

As Russell has suggested in the above quotation from him, the idea of the centrality of (heteronomous) work seems closely connected with the idea of the centrality of duty or obligation. Obligations are indeed themselves constraints;

and those under the spell of 'the morality system', as Williams calls it, see their lives as built around these. Work has traditionally been one of our central life-constraining obligations – originally religious, later secular-moral. The belief in the centrality of work owes its baselessness to the superordinate baselessness of the centrality of moral obligation.

Britain is currently taking a 'historical deep breath' in many related aspects of its national life. The traditional pillars of its culture, for a century and more pitted by scepticism, are now half eaten away. Organised religion is on a statistical path towards extinction (White, 1995, p 3, 19). With each new younger generation the 'peculiar institution' of morality, in sexual matters not least, comes to seem more and more irrelevant, personal fulfilment and intimate attachments coming to be far more prized. National sentiment in its familiar form seems to be going a similar way, although what should replace it is very unclear.

The same may be beginning to be true of the doctrine of work. Thatcherism, here as in the other areas, has been a catalyst to reflection. No one could miss its rescue-operation on traditional morality, the Christian faith, the British character and the work-ethic. In putting the political spotlight on these, it invited fundamental thought about them. Traditional attitudes which may otherwise have continued to live on unnoticed for years on the cultural seabed bubbled to the surface – not least in the Falklands War. Their greater visibility has prompted a more thoroughgoing reassessment.

The centrality of work has recently come under challenge from various directions. First, the widespread belief that the high rates of unemployment, which have now been with us for many years, are not really comparable with those in the interwar slump. They are becoming accepted as an apparently permanent phenomenon. This is reflected in recent Labour Party draft manifestos, which have dropped the symbolic socialist words 'full employment' (*The Independent*, 5 July 1996). Many people across the social classes are now not employed at all, or opting for voluntary work in areas of personal interest, often for a pittance, or are having to make do with part-time work – sometimes by choice, or are urged into early retirement. Non-workers or semi-workers, many if not all of whom are able to fill their free time with enjoyable activities of their own choosing, are becoming a more familiar part of the social scene. The proportion of pensioners in the society is increasing as people are living longer. If for this last reason we can now expect a fifth to a quarter of our lives to be free from (heteronomous) work (including schoolwork), rather than half this amount or less two or three generations ago, this must further help to whittle away the idea that life is virtually all work. Among those in work, flexi-working, which is on the increase, tends to make the demands of paid employment subordinate to personal concerns, rather than vice-versa. In addition, the assumption that a job is for life, which has prevailed in many sectors, has been thoroughly undermined in the last few years. Tenure has disappeared in universities and elsewhere; people are encouraged from schooldays onwards to expect to change their jobs several times in their lifetime and to seek appropriate retraining. This seems likely to threaten the notion of a lifetime 'vocation' embedded in our work culture since the Puritans' insistence on what God has called each of us to do in his service. Philosophically, the post-Christian concept of a 'life-plan' is now increasingly seen as a detachable part of personal flourishing; and outside philosophy, in understandable reaction to the uncertain economic future, more and more people seem to think less of a lifetime 'career' than a more flexible way of life, sensitive to changing circumstances. Philosophically again, the last decade's critique of an obligation-centred ethics may both reflect and encourage wider currents of thought with a similar content, *inter alia* weakening the depiction of work as a central duty in our lives.

Perhaps mirroring some of the trends picked out in the last paragraph, a recent article in *The Independent* (11 May 1995), headlined *'In no hurry to get a job'*, states that a survey of final-year students at British universities shows that a majority of them do not expect to start work when they finish their course and that many of them have a desultory attitude to applying for jobs while they are still studying. A representative of the employers' organisation, the Association of Graduate Recruiters, expressed his concern 'about the relatively small amount of effort a number of graduates appear to be putting into something that can shape their destiny'.

NOTES

1. I am assuming here that Marx's 'creative work' is roughly equivalent to what I have called 'autonomous work'. This assumption may be challengeable.

THREE

Work and well-being

INTRODUCTION

I turn now from critique to a constructive account of the place of work in a human life, particularly in advanced industrial societies like Britain and other countries. I shall not start with an alleged need to work, or right to work, or obligation to work. We need to begin further back, with what it is for a person to lead a flourishing life. Only then can we see what place work in its various forms – autonomous and heteronomous – might have in this.

HUMAN WELL-BEING

I introduced the notion of flourishing, or personal well-being, in Chapter 1, when discussing the definition of work. We saw there that a life can be said to be more flourishing, the more the agent's major goals in life are fulfilled. We also saw the salience in modern culture of autonomous well-being, that is, where one's major goals are self-chosen rather than imposed from the outside.

Autonomous flourishing should be distanced from two other notions which it might seem natural to build into it.

It does not require a plan of life. Some philosophers, notably John Rawls (1971, ch 7), have assumed that this is a matter of progressively realising long-term plans. But this overlooks individual differences in the way individuals approach their lives, some being more forward-looking and others more spontaneous. It also overlooks the fact that people can lead flourishing lives in tradition-directed societies, where the idea of planning one's life gets no purchase. While it is true that a human life, even in a tradition-directed society, would be impossible without having some sort of future objectives in mind and working out ways of realising them, this may apply only to things like making good tools or building a wall to keep away wild animals; it need have nothing to do with delineating the future contours of a large part of one's life as a whole. The notion of 'life-planning' is connected with those of 'vocation' and 'career' (see also below, p 94). It is not essential to human flourishing, and hence to autonomous flourishing.

Secondly, the 'major goals' which enter into the notion of well-being and *a fortiori* autonomous well-being do not necessitate end-products. The distinction here is between goals that do involve these, like building a wall or writing a novel or solving some kind of personal problem, and those that do not, like listening to Gershwin, spending an evening in the pub with friends, making love, walking in the country. All these latter four are activity-related goals, although unlike the earlier cases, the activities need not, and typically do not, generate end-products: they can be and are usually engaged in solely for intrinsic features of the activities themselves. But not all major goals need have to do with activities (of either sort). It may be important to one to be a certain sort of person: one who tries to live up to their ideals, for instance, or someone well-disposed or helpful. *Being* as well as doing can constitute a goal. So can reactive dispositions like wanting attention or recognition. These distinctions are relevant to the place of work in human life. Both autonomous and heteronomous work incorporate the idea of an end-product. This reminds us – which we already knew well enough – that one's major goals in life need not be achievable through work. They may also encompass: intrinsic delights of activities without end-products, like reading fiction or swimming in the sea; character-goals, like being reliable or fair in one's dealings with others; reactive goals, like wanting fame or to be loved, feared or revered.

These last examples remind us that people's major goals as autonomous agents are not always ethically benign: Stalin's repressive empire was built round his master-wish to be universally feared; Hitler wanted to demean and exterminate the Jews and Slavs. In taking autonomous flourishing as a starting-point for what I shall be saying about the place of work and of education for work, I shall be assuming certain ethical constraints on it. In social and educational policy we are not about cultivating a nation of Hitlers or Stalins, or even, on lesser rungs on the scale of inhumanity or selfishness, individuals animated by *Schadenfreude*, the desire to dominate or to gain attention. Enjoying attention or recognition is not necessarily bad in itself. On the contrary, we reinforce such common, probably organically-rooted, desires by building everyday devices of recognition into the fabric of social interaction. It is only when this enjoyment becomes unbalanced, when people begin to crave recognition, fame, notoriety out of all proportion, that we look at it askance. In what follows I shall be assuming a concept of autonomous well-being that includes a genuine care for others' flourishing as well as one's own, and rules out exaggerated preoccupation with the latter.

Basic needs

In giving this thumbnail account of an individual's well-being, I have concentrated so far on goals and desires, but something should also be said about needs. Each of us, as an animal entity, has certain organic needs, whose satisfaction or non-satisfaction is vitally important to our well-being. Any human being needs to eat and drink, eliminate, breathe, operate within certain extremes of temperature, have some kind of shelter. These things do not necessarily constitute goals: taking in oxygen is something we have to do, but it is not something at which we aim.

What are needs? One cannot understand them in the abstract, only as related to something for which they are needed. In the present context, this is physical survival as an organism. Air, food and water are necessary to this survival. In general, X is a need in relation to Y if X is necessary to Y, that is, if Y could not exist without X. This general schema applies to all kinds of cases, including those of a humdrum, everyday sort, like someone's need for a stamp in order to post a letter. Survival needs are obviously more fundamental and as such are more intimately connected with personal well-being. One can flourish without posting letters or postage stamps, but not without what is necessary for survival.

Sometimes when people write about 'human needs' or 'basic human needs', they embrace not only bare survival needs. We have already encountered several accounts of work as a basic human need: Norman's, Doyal and Gough's, and Sayers'. None of these writes about work (in some sense) as a condition of mere survival. The reference point seems, rather, to be some kind of notion of human well-being: Norman's 'meaningful work', Doyal and Gough's 'participation in the division of labour', and Sayers' 'socially productive labour' are held to be necessary to human flourishing.

Whether or not these specific claims are true takes us back over ground already covered – to what might be meant by 'work' and other terms; to the presence or absence of grounds for the claims; and to counterexamples of apparently flourishing people who do not lift a finger. The more important question for our present purposes is what, if anything, might constitute basic human needs in relation to personal flourishing as distinct from bare survival?

Plainly this cannot be answered without first establishing what personal flourishing is. I have said something about this above, starting from a very abstract account of this in terms of the satisfaction of major goals and then honing this into an account suitable for our times by building into it requirements of autonomy and ethical benignness. The more abstract account already brings in its train needs beyond those for mere survival. To take just one example, whether or not possessing language is a condition of survival, it is certainly necessary for the hierarchical arrangement of goals implicit in the notion of 'major goals' and perhaps in the concept of human personhood itself. Acquiring language thus becomes a human well-being need in general. With more determinate notions of well-being, linguistic needs also become more specific. Where tribesmen needed only to speak and understand the language of their tribe, autonomous agents of a modern state like Britain need also to be literate: illiteracy tends to diminish one's level of well-being.

This pattern of argument, with its distinction between abstract well-being needs and well-being needs appropriate to our own kind of society, can be applied more generally – to education, for instance. This is a well-being need in any society, in that children have to be brought up in the values, beliefs and practices of their social group in order to flourish as adult members of it. In a society like contemporary Britain the basic need for education takes more particular shape. Children have to be equipped with ethical dispositions and attitudes peculiar to a liberal democratic polity; and have also to understand something of the workings and historical roots of a complex industrialised society, the kinds of life-options available to them within it as potentially autonomous persons, and much else besides. All these things become seen as indispensable elements in a worthwhile life.

In other spheres the same distinction applies. Between a more general notion of health as a condition of well-being and our own more specific requirements, inconceivable without scientific advances, such as the availability of dental care and surgery under anaesthetic. Between some kind of shelter and what we would now take to be a minimum standard of decent housing. Between social recognition unspecified and the variegated patterns appropriate to our different spheres of social interaction – as friends, relatives, neighbours, colleagues and strangers. I need not labour the point further. In these and other spheres, what counts as a basic need is not tightly circumscribed, but can be expected to change with changing social circumstances. In late twentieth century Britain no one can get by without relying at some point on mechanised transport or the telephone – something not true at all of people living here a century ago. In the next generation the home computer may, for all we know, be perceived as similarly indispensable.

If social and educational policy is to be directed towards enhancing individual well-being, there are good grounds for filling this out in the more determinate ways suggested in the last two sections – towards putting everyone in a position to achieve their major goals as autonomous, ethically sensitive agents and towards satisfying the preconditions of this in the form of human needs basic to our kind of life.

AUTONOMOUS WORK

What place does autonomous work have in the good life as just sketched? We defined this earlier as a form of activity whose end-product is chosen as a major goal of an autonomous agent. It can be paid or unpaid. If it is paid, then it is not merely chosen as the best option given that one has to earn a living, but as something one would prefer to do even if one did not have to earn a living. Given that autonomy can be of different degrees, it is helpful to think in terms of a range of cases. Imagine first a journalist with a private income for whom writing articles is a major goal. She is paid for her contributions, but does not need the money. Next, someone who chooses to become a nurse, needs the money from her work, but would still choose to nurse even if she had a private income. Both journalist and nurse are nearer to the ideal of the autonomous worker than someone who wouldn't have chosen her job as a nurse if she didn't have to, but who, given that she has to have some sort of job, prefers nursing to other alternatives and places the proper pursuit of her job high in her value-hierarchy. She, in her turn, is closer to the ideal than someone who, having to have a job, equally prefers nursing, but only 'as the best of a bad job', performing its duties without commitment, simply to earn a wage. The latter can hardly be counted as an example of autonomous work at all.

The end-products of autonomous work can be goods and services useful to other people; goods of personal significance to oneself; or more impersonal goods.

Among goods and services useful to others are those which help to satisfy their basic needs. Since this part of the paper examines the place of work in human life in a very general way, we must be careful not to write into the framework occupational structures as we now know them. There is a danger that we have just done this by talking about nursing as paid employment. But the danger is minimal in this instance. If we could abstract from present work structures to an idealised situation in which ethically-sensitive autonomous agents were choosing their preferred goals, it is likely that some people would be drawn towards caring for the sick. We can safely say this, knowing that health is a basic human need and knowing that people brought up to care for others' well-being will be concerned with this as a specific object of this care. We can reasonably assume, too, that health care cannot be left to individuals acting independently but has to be organised into complex occupational structures.

The same moves can be made for other forms of autonomous work – bringing up children, teaching, farming, designing and making houses, clothes, furniture and other necessities, activities centred around giving people their due to do with law or administration, or those more directly responsive to people's need to live together in a political community.

The examples given are mainly to do with basic human needs, interpreting this broadly to include not only bare survival needs but also well-being needs applicable to a modern liberal-democratic society. We can safely assume that many of our idealised autonomous agents will be interested in doing autonomous work aimed at meeting such needs.

Others among them will want autonomous work still in the sphere of promoting others' flourishing but targeted now on meeting preferences rather than needs. I have in mind that part of personal flourishing which has to do with satisfying one's major goals. Someone may want to play clarinet in an orchestra but not have a basic need to do this. Again, there should be no shortage of volunteers to work as clarinet-makers, clarinet teachers, conductors of orchestras, concert organisers and so on. Other people are keen gardeners, film-goers, squash-players, photographers .... The opportunities for autonomous work to meet these preferences are legion – remembering always that the work done must constitute a major goal of the worker himself or herself: it is done not simply to earn a living, as a mere means to an end, but as something important to one in the overall structuring of one's life.

Generally then, we can conclude that in an ideal world many autonomous agents would be likely to opt for activities which met others' needs or satisfied their more important goals. They would still be engaged in these as autonomous agents even if they earned a living by them, given that they chose them not primarily for this reason but because they formed a part of their ideal pattern of life. In a large-scale society like our own many of these forms of autonomous work would have to be organised into bureaucratic structures.

Autonomous work can be directed to one's own ends, as well as other people's. Tending one's garden, for instance, or decorating one's house. Once again, I am assuming agents for whom these are major goals. The agents' goals in question in these examples, by the way, are not having a well-looked-after garden or nicely decorated house, but – from the agent's viewpoint – *my* looking after my garden, *my* decorating my house. No doubt in our *tabula rasa* society many would opt for autonomous work in this more personal category.

Finally, there is autonomous work whose end-products are not connected with oneself, in the way that one's house or garden is so connected, but are more impersonal goods. Examples would be intellectual products, like philosophical or scientific theories, biographies or histories. Works of art range between personal and impersonal end-products depending on such things as their expressive, as distinct from their formal, content. Some people would choose autonomous work in this third category, probably fewer than those choosing it from the first two.

Does this exhaust the types of autonomous work? In Chapter 1 we looked at various attractive features of some jobs as we know them, those which can cause them to be labelled 'good' jobs. I am thinking here of such things as the trappings of high status; opportunities for social interaction and social recognition; power over subordinates; high salaries and pension packages; private health benefits; company cars; business lunches or ample breaks; a physically pleasant working environment; generous leave; wide scope for decision-making. Suppose, as is likely, some of those who now do jobs carrying with them benefits like these would be willing to do them assuming they were idealised autonomous agents, i.e. without the constraint of having to earn a living. (We would have to subtract from the benefits the financial ones.) According to the criterion introduced earlier,would their jobs not then fall under our category of autonomous work?

Not necessarily. Autonomous work requires agents to have among their self-chosen major goals the goal of producing something. The autonomous nurse helps to restore health or provide comfort; the autonomous carpenter makes cabinets and armchairs. What would someone working in a 'good' job like a senior manager in a canned peas firm be producing? Well, clearly, he would be helping to produce canned peas. But would helping to produce canned peas be among the major goals of his life from the idealised standpoint? Very probably not. Would some more general description of this, like helping to produce food for people, be among them? Again, quite possibly not. Suppose what attracts him to his job, what makes it so fulfilling that he would want to do it even if his income came from elsewhere, is high status or power over others. These are not necessarily connected with producing peas. He could have got them in a bank, an insurance company, a firm making computer parts. Neither, more to the point, are such goals end-product goals. Wanting high status is a species of wanting social recognition: one's goal – in this example, as is so often the case in the real world, a major goal – is that others should look up to one, pay one attention, perhaps envy one; it is not, as with the carpenter or nurse, to produce some kind of good or service which others need or want. The motivation is self-referential, not other-directed. The same is true of wanting power over others.

Autonomous work does not automatically embrace autonomous activity in work (see above, p 10). Unless other candidates are suggested, it should be restricted to the three sub-categories already detailed.

Let us turn from logical to ethical matters. What place does autonomous work have in personal well-being, in a flourishing life? Is it a necessary feature of it? Do we have a need for autonomous work?

We should look again at those philosophers who argue for work as a human need. Two of the three 'needs-based' texts we have looked at, by Doyal and Gough, and by Sayers, do not seem to focus exclusively, or perhaps even mainly, on *autonomous* work. Doyal and Gough write of 'deliberate participation in the overall division of labour' as a basic need, but one can participate in this without one's work being autonomous. Sayers seems close to their view in his frequent equation of working with having a job, so the same can be said about his position. In a revealing bracket he writes that 'work (at least of any but the most repulsive and degrading sort) is also now felt subjectively as a need. ... it is a vital want, a need' (p 741). Work which is not repulsive or degrading seems to cover much more than autonomous work alone.

Of the three writers, Norman comes closest to arguing that it is specifically autonomous work which constitutes a human need. He claims that we all have a need for 'meaningful unalienated work'. If we take the first of these two adjectives, we can ask whether meaningful work is necessarily autonomous. This depends, of course, on what is being written into 'meaningful'. For Adina Schwartz, this is work which is not mechanical, which requires the exercise of one's intelligence and allows one to participate in decision-making. As we saw, she believes everyone has a right to such work deriving from their right to lead an autonomous life. In discussing her views, I questioned whether a worker who came up to her requirements of meaningfulness – in being employed, for instance, in manufacturing supermarket trolleys – was necessarily engaged in autonomous work. This would only be the case if she had chosen making trolleys as a major goal in her life, as something to which she attached great personal importance. If, as is likely, many people in her position would not do this, meaningful work would not necessarily be autonomous work. Whether Norman has the same understanding as Schwartz of 'meaningful work' is not clear, although it must at least be non-mechnical and in some sense creative. In any case, what he claims as a human need is meaningful *unalienated* work. He writes of Marx's ideas that:

> when work has this character, when it is meaningful, creative and self-expressive … it constitutes the organising centre of a person's life, it gives the individual a sense of his or her own identity, recognised and confirmed by others, and it calls forth his or her energies and capacities. Alienated labour lacks these qualities. It lacks them when it becomes simply the earning of a wage, with no intrinsic significance for the worker, an activity over which he has no say and into which he puts nothing of himself. (p 175)

Although he is here writing about Marx, perhaps we would be justified as reading this also as Norman's own view and therefore as showing more fully what he takes to be a basic human need. Assuming this, the kind of work he has in mind does seem to be autonomous: as it is of considerable personal significance to the worker it looks as if it must have been chosen as a major goal, as something intrinsically important and not at all a replaceable means to some further end.

If this is the claim – that autonomous work is a human need, is necessary to our flourishing – then what are the grounds for it? In our earlier discussion of Norman we noted the weakness in his position here. Norman apart, how could one establish this in the face of the well-known plurality of items which could be included in a list of major personal goals? Autonomous work is one possible ingredient in the good life, but it has its legitimate competitors. As well as artistic creation, craft activity or social service, there are activities like cycling, religious contemplation, walking on the downs, listening to music and eating out. None of these need involve producing any kind of end-product; all of them could be among a person's major commitments. In addition to activities, major goals may also include desires to be a certain sort of person – to be friendly and courteous, fairminded, a man or woman of principle. If not all major goals are work-goals, *must* the latter figure among any particular person's major goals? Could one autonomously build a life around non-work?

Agreed, many, almost certainly most, of us, given the power to choose, probably *would* go for end-product goals, at least as part of the total package. But there is, as far as I can see, no necessity for us to do so: what mix we adopt is – within limits, to exclude the ethically suspect – up to us. G E Moore's 'Bloomsbury' ideal of life, as described in *Principia Ethica*, revolved around the enjoyment of beauty and intimate personal relationships (Moore, 1903). Work, even autonomous work, had no place in it. In some versions of the spiritual life, everything is subordinated to contemplation of the divine. Autonomous work may be something which perhaps nearly all of us would want to include in our lives in some way; but it does not seem to be strictly a need.

A possible objection here might be that although one can imagine lives which are both workless and flourishing, this could only be on some restricted notion of flourishing which did not require much, if any, concern for the well-being of others. Rich self-centred fainéants may find fulfilment in a round of pleasures. The Bloomsbury ideal insists at least on intimate relationships, but its altruistic sensitivities evaporate beyond the salon and the sitting room. If we are working with a notion of autonomous well-being which has written into it a responsiveness to the needs and aspirations of others across the national community and beyond, will this not necessarily include among its major goals wanting to serve others in some way – attending to their physical or other needs, or helping them to realise important goals? If so, will not autonomous well-being embrace within it autonomous work?

Not necessarily. Even if one spends part of one's life working for others, this need not be *autonomous* work – even if one is an autonomous agent. One may autonomously choose to make supermarket trolleys or paperclips where these products have no personal significance for one, but where the money one earns enables one to lead a decent life, attentive to others' needs and wants as well as one's own.

Pressing for autonomous work to be an indispensable element of the good life ignores the elasticity of the latter concept, the very many forms it can take. This is important educationally, as insisting to young people on the indispensability of autonomous work limits their possibilities. There is even less reason to believe that autonomous work must be *central* to a human life. Some people will want it to be in their own case, but others will prefer a variety of types of major goal to such monomania. In Isaiah Berlin's terminology, most of us are foxes, few hedgehogs. Social policy should reflect this and not make autonomous work in any form the dominating feature of everyone's life. It should make possible, and encourage, the availability of a wide variety of ways of life in which it might – or might not – find a place.

HETERONOMOUS WORK

For many, it would be an ideal world if the only work anyone ever did were autonomous – that is, would be among their major preferences even if they did not have to depend on it for an income. But the real world is not like that. Drains have to be laid, roads repaired, carpets hoovered, buses driven, business letters typed. In any modern society all sorts of jobs have to be done which few would wish to do unless they had to. Some heteronomous work is unavoidable. (I shall use 'heteronomous work' henceforth to mean 'heteronomous work

which is personally non-significant'. The fact that this excludes the heteronomous work of the traditional peasant (see above, p 6) is not important, given
that our framework is the well-being of autonomous people). But if the social
ideal is that every individual should lead a flourishing life, there is a good reason for making whatever heteronomous work there has to be as compatible as
possible with this. How should one proceed?

This is not the place to go into specifics. But our earlier discussion has
implications which it will be helpful to draw out now, if only in a sketchy way.
The first is that heteronomous work, as constrained, is *prima facie* in conflict
with the ideal of an autonomous life and would seem, again *prima facie*, to
diminish one's well-being rather than promote it. Is the way forward, then, to
try to reduce its overall amount to a minimum? This does not strictly follow,
because a job's *prima facie* disbenefits might be outweighed by financial or
psychological advantages attached to it – if, for instance, an otherwise unattractive job earned one extremely high wages for two or three hours' work a
day. But it would seem desirable, if not to reduce it to a minimum, at least to
reduce it, especially because the *prima facie* drawbacks are unlikely to be coun-
tered in this way in very many cases. If Britain and comparable societies were
rich enough to pay most people extremely high wages for low-hours jobs which
went against the grain, it would be a different story – as it would be if we had
kept the centrality assumption: the sensible policy then would have been to
create conditions to enable everyone to work a full stint, autonomously or
heteronomously. With the centrality notion now behind us, a progressive
reduction in heteronomous work would seem the best way forward.

This suggestion is still based on at least two further assumptions: one, that,
freed from the centrality notion, some people brought up to be autonomous
would tend to rate more time to themselves as a high priority; two, that the
total amount of heteronomous work *can* be reduced without threatening the
society's well-being. The first of these is an empirical claim based, pretty
securely, I would hope, on experience of human nature. The second also seems
empirically to be the case. However one fills in the details – and there will be
value-conflicts between different fillers-in at various points – there is likely to
be broad agreement that some heteronomous work is more essential than other
kinds and that somewhere towards the less essential end of the scale, some is
removable altogether.

How far and in what ways heteronomous work can be cut down takes us
beyond philosophical territory. It takes us into technological studies, for
instance, about scope for further automation. This said, all the signs are that
the massive advances in automative technology over the last half-century will
continue unabated into the next.

There are three points to make about the reducibility of heteronomous
work, which rest on philosophical points.

Heteronomous work can range from highly-paid managerial jobs to others
that are tedious and boring; it can also vary in enjoyability. The three points

depend on one or other of these distinctions.

[1] My first focus is on the 'top' end of the labour market. In discussing autonomous work I mentioned people like some senior managers who have no personal interest in the product (canned peas, bug guns), but do attach major value to the power, status, attention, recognition which their job brings. The issue is: is there a point beyond which attachment to goals of this sort becomes ethically unacceptable?

The desire for social recognition, to take this first, is a deep-set feature of human life. Perhaps rooted biologically in something like desires for attention found in other primates and in household pets, this takes human form in the way we go out of our way not to ignore people, to show them we are aware of their presence, approve of what they say, do and are. Recognition seems to be a fundamental human need, perhaps even for survival, certainly for any kind of flourishing existence (White, 1994).

It is a need, but not necessarily a goal. We give each other tokens of esteem and we all welcome these when we receive them, but we do not for that reason *aim* at receiving them. They are, for the most part, embedded in the taken-for-granted background of our social life. Sometimes they are more than this – goals as well as things that happen to us. Very often this is nothing to raise an ethical eyebrow, or not much of one. The little vanities of amateur painters who have their sights on the summer exhibition in the local library are among the tolerable weaknesses of everyday existence. But aiming at recognition as a central objective in one's life is in a different category. It is risky from the point of view of one's own well-being, however broadly conceived, as it is likely to make one excessively dependent on the continued attentiveness of other people. If we restrict the notion of well-being to the ethically sensitive version with which we have been working in this paper, it is hard to see how recognition-seeking of any substantial sort could be included, as it *demands* from others what they should be willingly according. Sometimes this is, as it were, an unenforceable demand: a would-be celebrity as a comedian would *like* large crowds to laugh at her jokes, but cannot insist on this. Our senior manager has the equivalent of a captive audience, being able to put pressure on his subordinates to give him the esteem that he lives for ... or else. This contravenes the social ideal of autonomous well-being, as the subordinates are being constrained to have – or at least appear to have – goals which they otherwise probably would not have chosen. For this reason, wanting high status in one's job is not ethically acceptable as a major goal.

Wanting power over others, to take another motive driving our imagined manager, can also come in benigner forms, as part of some larger enterprise. A schoolteacher, intent on getting her pupils to learn, will want them to do what she says in various ways. But she does not want power for its own sake, and *a fortiori* not as a major life-goal. As the latter, it is open to the same criticism as seeking high status: both involve getting others to do things which they might not otherwise want to do; in the case of high status this is giving the status-seeker a lot of attention and esteem, while with power it consists in doing whatever it is one is directed to do. Where the desire for power or status has elements of *Schadenfreude*, of delighting in the distress that one is causing in others – in evoking in them pain or fear or envy, perhaps – its ethical unacceptability is even plainer. This, too, can be a feature of our occupational culture.

The connexion of these remarks with the issue of work-reduction should be plain. If jobs which depend on excessive attachment to social recognition and power are ethically deficient, this provides one reason for removing them or altering them so as to eliminate their shortcomings. How far this points in a Schwarzian direction towards undermining the distinction between managers and managed or towards a more upright conception of the manager I do not know.

[2] I'd like to come back to Dahrendorf's surprise (see p 15 above) at finding how much many British people as compared with other Europeans enjoy their long hours at work.

> At first sight, there is a strange paradox about work in Britain. On the one hand, it consumes a greater part of people's lives than in most comparable countries; on the other hand, people seem to work much less hard than elsewhere. Work for most is still the centre of their lives. If ever there was a work society, it is Britain. One is not surprised to learn … that the average Briton worked, in 1980, 238 hours more than the average Continental European. … The other side of the picture is that one lives at work, that is to say, one does not go to work in order to work, but in order to spend an agreeable day. (Dahrendorf, 1982, pp 45–46)

Dahrendorf makes it clear in a passage quoted earlier that he is not being critical in writing this. 'What we are describing is one of the reasons for the very pleasantness of life in Britain which is so widely, and so rightly, admired' (ibid.). I take his point. Not only in Britain, if especially there, do people enjoy the concomitant benefits which can accrue from being at work – good company, mutual recognition and so on. I feel Dahrendorf may be seeing things just a little through rose-coloured – or maybe red-white-and-blue-coloured – spectacles. It is not as though people have autonomously chosen this pattern of life over all alternatives. They have to work. Their culture has made work central to their lives and it can be pretty dull. As I suggested in Chapter 1, they have accepted the inevitable and injected into it some personal fulfilment. If working were not a financial necessity for them, would they prefer to attain these forms of fulfilment through a life filled with heteronomous work, or in some other way? If asked now, I imagine many would choose the latter – not necessarily wanting to be totally free from heteronomous work, but preferring more time to themselves to pursue other things. If so, this would suggest that the total volume of heteronomous work might be pared away so as to match these ideal preferences more closely. People would see more clearly that the work they had been doing was a replaceable means to other ends.

Answers to the question just posed – about how far people would still want heteronomous work if they had alternative income – would be likely to reflect the influence of the centrality doctrine. Preferences for abundant heteronomous work might well be more numerous than they would have been if respondents had a fuller understanding of the origins and place of the doctrine in the culture, as well as a fuller ethical understanding of the components of their own well-being.

[3] My third comment is about unpleasant work – i.e. work which is mechanical, exhausting, dangerous or boring. The case for reducing this in the interests of personal well-being is overwhelming. There is no need to labour the familiar point that in a society like ours a lot of work like this goes into producing goods and services superfluous to people's basic needs and uncoerced preferences, goods and services which depend on mass advertising to get us to want them. The wastefulness of our consumer society heaps up behind it a quite unnecessary mountain of heteronomous work. Individual well-being can be dealt a double blow: the temptations and pressures of consumerism can knock consumers' value-hierarchy out of kilter; and can oblige themselves or others as producers to spend too much of their lives in thrall to labouring.

What do I mean by 'knock their value-hierarchy out of kilter'? Let me re-introduce yet again the notion of 'major goals'. Our goals are arranged in a systematic hierarchy of importance, the major ones at the top being of greatest significance and generally winning out over less important goals where conflicts occur between them. A major goal in my own case would be thinking philosophically; a minor one, eating out in restaurants. I could give up the latter if I had to, but not the former. It is not that eating out has no value for me: it contributes, like a mass of other less weighty pursuits, to my overall well-being. But it must find its proper place in my whole psychic economy, yielding to the things that matter to me more when this is appropriate and trumping things of lesser value.

Upbringing, on this account of well-being, has much to do with psychic regulation. Our substantive dispositions to desire different ends at different levels in the hierarchy are kept in proper relationship to each other by structural dispositions whose role it is to do this. These dispositions are called 'virtues'. Virtues also have other roles – in regulating feelings as well as desires, although in practice the two typically come together. The virtue of self-control has to do with managing our feelings of anger and associated desires to retaliate. There is a place for legitimate anger in our lives (some people, especially some women, perhaps do not allow themselves to feel angry enough), but excessive anger can get in the way of other projects. Hence our need for this virtue.

Among desires and associated feelings we need to regulate are bodily appetites for food, drink and sex. The virtue here is temperance. Again, these desires are fine in themselves: the pleasures which their satisfaction brings can contribute greatly to our well-being. But however urgent, these satisfactions are by no means always the most important of our goals and have often to cede to those which are. This is sometimes difficult for us, seeing how insistent these appetites can be. Hence our need for temperance.

Another part of our original constitution, it would seem, is the desire for social recognition discussed above. Like the desire for food, there is nothing ethically amiss with it in itself. The little signs of mutual esteem we give each other are part of the normal background of human intercourse and help us all to flourish better. But, like the desire for food, it can get out of hand, turning, as the latter turns into greed, into excessive desires for attention or celebrity. In both cases, important goals can be threatened or elbowed aside. We do not have a special name for the virtue which keeps recognition in order (and even with the bodily appetites we have only the philosophers' oddity 'temperance', so easily confused with the anti-alcoholic sense of the term). 'Humility' comes close, except that it brings with it dispensable Christian associations.

Our consumerist society is a culture of temptation. Newspapers, magazines, television and advertisements fill our value-horizons with the imagined delights of status, sex, food and drink, as goods either in their own right or associated with some other product. More general than these is the temptation to acquire goods as such, almost as an end in itself – as when we feel we cannot leave Our Price or Waterstones or Next empty-handed, even though we have seen nothing we want. I have no figures on how far people are swayed towards these ends or how far they are tempted by them away from what are for them worthwhile goals. If, as seems likely from impressionistic evidence, as well as from the billions which media barons continue to pour into all this, these temptations and diversions *are* significant, how does this bear on the issue of work-reduction?

In this way: people buy masses of goods and services not because they need them, or in order to lead a fuller life, but out of temptation. If we were all better equipped to understand and withstand these temptations, we would be less likely to want to buy things. If so, less unattractive heteronomous work would have to be engaged in to produce them.

All this helps, I hope, to explain what I meant by 'knocking value-hierarchies out of kilter.' As a further dimension of this, I come back to the centrality of work. This sixteenth century invention bids fair to persist into the twenty-first, thanks to consumerist obsessions which keep production at full stretch. The more one's life is taken up with heteronomous work, the less time and quietness one has to think about one's life and what makes it worthwhile. There is excess and deficiency in the latter as there is in all dispositions of character. Hamlet went too far. Too many of us in our hectic age do not go far enough. It is, of course, in the interests of those who produce and sell temptation goods that people lack the time and inclination to think things through properly. Keeping noses to grindstones brings more than one kind of benefit.

The sum total of heteronomous work could well be decreased: too much effort is spent on producing goods which people do not need or would not choose if they thought things through. Whether we could get by with an average of four hours' work a day, as Russell suggested, I do not know. But it would be good to see Britain systematically beginning to reduce working hours as some of its neighbours have done or intend to do. We have already seen in Dahrendorf the 238 hours that British people worked more than continental Europeans in 1980. Two more recent statistics: while the average hours usually worked per week in Britain remained almost stationary between 1986 and 1992, those worked in the Netherlands dropped by over six and a half hours (Central Statistical Office 1989, p 78; 1995, p 71). Polly Toynbee (1995) reports that British men 'work longer hours than in any other EC country, on average 44 hours a week. Sixty per cent of men work more than 40 hours, whereas in the rest of Europe fewer than half work that long, a third of British women work more than 40 hours, while only 14 per cent of women in the rest of Europe work so long.'

It would be good if Britain were to follow this continental lead.

If I am right about my hunch that Britain is taking a deep historical breath – and there is nothing like a new millenium (ten times better than a mere new century) to make us all sit back and wonder where we should be heading – then perhaps we can hope that the centrality of work will be taken less and less for granted. There are signs that this is happening already. People are getting used to new patterns of work and non-work – jobs that last a few years, not for life; part-time work, sometimes perforce, but sometimes to support one's other life as a singer-songwriter or jewellery-maker; flexitime; job-shares; early retirement, again often out of necessity, but also enhancing possibilities of autonomous living and working. The ice-floe doctrine of work's centrality may at last be breaking up.

The ecology movement may be helping it to do so. Everyone knows now that the world cannot continue to produce the raw materials on the scale required by consumerism this century. Everyone knows now about the pollution consumerism causes. Even if the ethical difficulties mentioned above about warped conceptions of well-being fail to change attitudes towards over-production, more tangible worries about the imminent future of oil supplies, forests and ozone layers may have more power to do so.

As Robert Dearden once remarked, ecological worries may have the philosophical consequence of causing us to rethink the concept of autonomous flourishing. We may need to trim our goals in life to those which are planetarily affordable, bringing children up to weigh less environmentally harmful pursuits more heavily among possible options. Just as ethical constraints on possible goals should discourage a life of crime or prestige-seeking, so ecological constraints should turn them away from globally costlier lifestyles.

The ecological movement is one aspect of a larger recoil against the utilitarian approach to the economy which emphasises the *maximisation* of welfare and is manifested in companies' and governments' efforts to increase output, growth, profits, GNP without limit. Over the last twenty years philosophers have subjected utilitarian ethics to radical criticism. Its maximising assumption that the supreme ethical principle is that the *greatest* happiness ought to be produced has been shown to be without foundation, thinkers like Michael Slote (1989) arguing for 'satisficing' policies – which call for people having *enough* of life's goods – rather than 'optimising' approaches which demand the best possible. As Bernard Williams (1985, p 178) has argued, utilitarian moral theory is at least a marginal member of the 'morality system' (see above, p 43), which makes moral obligations central to our lives. If the notion that our supreme moral duty – as individuals or as a society – is to maximise the general happiness is under challenge, equally threatened is the obligation we may feel to work as hard as possible to bring about this end. The centrality of work in individuals' lives and in social policy may, with luck, be replaced in both spheres by the centrality of a satisfactory life for all.

This concludes the three philosophically-related points I wanted to make about the possibility of reducing heteronomous work. I turn now to more general conclusions.

TOWARDS THE ACTIVITY SOCIETY

What place should work have in our lives in the twenty-first century? There are two opposed answers.

The first continues to assume that (largely heteronomous) work should be central. This will be increasingly unlikely if older employment patterns decay either through economic pressures or through declining attachments to the ideologies which have supported the centrality thesis: Christianity, traditional morality, one strand in socialism, market economics. But the very breadth of support for the thesis across the spiritual and political spectrum and its ancient embeddedness within British culture make it difficult to undermine quickly. As Dahrendorf (1982, p 185) says, 'the work society will linger on, at least in official thinking and acting.' Current changes in employment patterns may in fact do as much to shore it up as to demolish it. The more people are unemployed or forced into retirement against their will, the greater the cachet attached to holding down an increasingly rare full-time job.

The second answer says that the centrality assumption needs to be challenged and the challenge translated into policy reforms. It has more radical and less radical versions.

To start with a revolutionary view: André Gorz, the French libertarian Marxist sociologist, has argued for 'a fundamentally different society'. (Gorz 1985, p 1). 'There can be no piecemeal solutions; the obstacles will only be overcome by overall restructuring, total transformation' (ibid.). His way forward consists in liberation from heteronomous work, by which he means 'socially productive labour' within the economic system as a whole. It is hetero-nomous because 'the social productive system can only operate like a single, giant machine, to which all the separate activities must be subordinate' (Gorz 1985, p 51), the scope for individual choice and initiative being thus severely restricted. Thanks to automation, it is now technically possible massively to reduce the amount of heteronomous work that has to be done to meet neces-sities. Gorz suggests it would be realistic if by the turn of the century everyone were expected to, and had the right to, do 20,000 hours of heteronomous work across his or her lifetime. ('It would be much less in an egalitarian society opt-ing for a less competitive, more relaxed way of life' (p 41).) How these hours would spread out across a lifetime could vary: they represent 10 years' full-time work, 20 years' part-time, 'or – a more likely choice – 40 years of inter-mittent work, part-time alternating with periods for holidays, or for unpaid autonomous activity, community work, etc.' (ibid.). In return for their 20,000 hours everyone would be assured of an income for life. In their new 'sphere of autonomy' people would be able to engage in the non-economic activities 'which are the very fabric of life itself. They encompass everything which is done, not for money, but out of friendship, love, compassion, concern; or for the satisfaction, pleasure and joy derived from activities themselves and from their end results' (p 48). Among these autonomous activities would be forms of small-scale and voluntary participation in the production of non-necessities at the level of the local community or smaller groups.

As someone who believes in work's centrality, Sean Sayers is, not surpris-ingly, sceptical about Gorz. In Sayers' view he is too hard on the work-ethic. This is not a ruling-class ideology, according to Sayers, but the reflection of a deeply felt human need at this stage of historical development (p 729). Although Gorz implicitly acknowledges this in the importance he attaches to the exercise of people's creative powers in autonomous work once liberated, he 'also argues that such fulfilment is possible only outside the sphere of employ-ment, which is unavoidably alienating' (p 730). But this is untrue. Although there are some menial and degrading jobs such that no one would willingly undertake them, most people 'gain genuine and important satisfactions from work' (p 731). In addition, Sayers agrees with the traditional labour movement view, as against Gorz, that 'leisure hours are a complement to work hours, not a substitute for them' (p 736, quoting M Jahoda *Employment and Unemployment*,Cambridge 1982, p 24).

I find myself between Gorz and Sayers. The former says the 'sphere of autonomy' should be central to life, the latter the sphere of paid employment. Both claims start too far in, with institutional structures rather than funda-mental values. I hope I have made plain my own starting-point: the autonomous well-being of each individual, where this has built into it a dimen-sion of concern for others' flourishing. It is *this* that should be central to life; it is a *subsidiary* issue how far and in what ways autonomous well-being requires engagement in autonomous work or liberation from heteronomous work.

A terminological difficulty needs clearing up. Gorz's use of the term 'heteronomous work' is significantly different from mine, as used in the last sentence for instance. For him it is 'work whose form and objectives are externally determined by the organisation of production on a national or continental scale' (p 50), in other words paid employment within the 'giant machine' of the economy. For me it is work where the agent has not chosen his or her participation in producing the end-product as one of his or her major goals in life. The two concepts do not coincide. Some of Gorz's heteronomous work could be autonomous in my terms – that is, where one's employment within the economic system, say as a nurse or journalist, is something one would have chosen as a major goal even if one did not depend on it as a source of income.

As Sayers rightly implies, Gorz wrongly associates personal fulfilment with liberation from employment within the economic system. In addition to the counterexample just mentioned – autonomous work within the system – we should not forget that autonomous agents can welcome heteronomous work (involving end-products which are of no personal significance as far as their major goals go, like supermarket trolleys or ironing boards) provided that its burdens are outweighed by its benefits viewed from the standpoint of autonomy. Gorz's 'sphere of autonomy' – which is defined not as a primordial phenomenon as is my 'autonomous well-being', but only in opposition to, and hence dependent on, the notion of heteronomous work in a Gorzian sense – is not what is central to human life. But admitting this does not commit one to agreeing with Sayers that paid employment is central. Centrality resides further back, at the level of basic values.

A word at this point about leisure and 'the leisure society'. If my last point is right, leisure should no more be at the heart of human life than the Marxist's or Puritan's 'work'. This seems to be true in whatever sense the word 'leisure' is taken. One sense is 'time free from work one is obliged or forced to do'. This does not introduce the notion of personal autonomy and can be applied *inter alia* to societies in which personal autonomy is virtually unknown. The Chinese film *Raising the Red Lantern* charts the relationships between four concubines of a local dignitary. Here, as in Jung Chang's description of her grandmother's early life as a war-lord's concubine in *Wild Swans* (Chang 1993, ch 1), we see how the concubine in that society, no doubt as a sign of her master's power and status, was expected to do no work but to live in idleness. But she was far from able to lead her own life, since everything she did was tightly prescribed by convention. Leisure in her case did not imply autonomy. There are no grounds for treating this kind of leisure as supremely important in human life.

Gorz's 'sphere of autonomy' is also a concept of leisure defined negatively in terms of freedom from constrained work in some sense. But being leisured now *does* imply being autonomous. As argued above, however, it would be mistaken to claim that Gorzian leisure should be central either.

The same goes for 'leisure' in the sense of recreation from work, where its prime function is to give people the energy and freshness to apply themselves to work once again. This follows from rejecting the centrality of work.

A fourth conception of leisure is the notion found in Aristotle of an area outside necessity-orientated work and made possible by it, devoted to pursuits worthwhile in themselves. In Aristotle's specific treatment of this in *Nicomachean Ethics* Book 10, the ideal use of leisure lies in contemplation of eternal truths. Is the more general conception here applicable to autonomous agents in our own day? Like Gorz's conception, this starts too far in and ungroundedly rules out necessity-orientated work as a possible major goal from the start. As Telfer points out, Aristotle's view demotes work too much (p 161). As she also says, there is no good reason for making contemplation the central activity (pp 158–160).

There is, finally, Telfer's own enlargement of the range of intrinsic goods in Aristotelian leisure to cover, besides the contemplation of necessary truths, the contemplation of beauty, discovery and creation and the enjoyment of personal relationships (ibid.). Telfer herself would not want to make leisure in this sense central to human life since she would not necessarily rate it higher in value than socially useful work.

To come back to the main argument. If Gorz's account of the future of work is flawed, what might replace it?

Philosophy can take one only so far. There are technological questions about how far automation is likely to continue to pare away work; as well as political and economic questions about how whatever work there is is to be distributed across the population. Philosophical considerations may well come in here but are not nearly enough on their own to generate policy decisions. With this *caveat*, what do they tell us?

What is central to an individual human life – that is, a life lived in a modern society based on liberal democratic principles – is not work of any kind, or leisure of any kind, but autonomous flourishing which is sensitive to others' needs and preferences. The hub of one's existence lies in the achievements, activities, passivities and relationships one pursues as one's major goals. Some of these have end-products and count as autonomous work; others lack these and do not count as work at all. There seems to be no overriding reason why work goals *must* figure prominently, or indeed at all, among one's major goals. At the same time, given the altruistic version of autonomous well-being with which we are working, one would expect most people to want to spend part of their time serving others in some way. More generally, given the ephemeral nature of human life and human beings' deeply-rooted desire to leave some however impermanent trace of themselves in all this transience, one would expect most people to direct some of their intelligence and energy into productive activity: few are likely to feel fulfilled by a life consisting wholly of non-productive pleasures – although, granted, some – van Parijs's surfers and others – may be.

All this brings me close to Ralf Dahrendorf's conception of the 'activity society' which he would like to see replacing the 'work society'. He is writing about Britain, but his point has more general application. 'Activity', for Dahrendorf, 'is human action which is freely chosen, which offers opportunities for self-expression, which carries satisfaction in itself, which is autonomous' (p 183). Technological advances are pressing us into a world where 'the work society is running out of work' (p 182). We cannot cling on to old ways, but should embrace the opportunities for greater human fulfilment that are now possible. Not only will there be more job-free time to spend on activities: jobs themselves:

> can be so transformed that they offer chances of activity. What has come to be called the humanisation of work is a major issue of social policy. Not only the world of production, but above all that of services is badly in need of an enlargement of the scope for human expression and initiative. Work need not be heteronomous, an unwanted and imposed burden, if we put our minds to bringing about the necessary changes. (p 184)

As we saw earlier, Dahrendorf is as impressed by, as much as he is critical of, the laid-back attitudes to their jobs he perceives among the British. Our tradition of making our work as pleasant as possible is something on which we can capitalise in the new world. I would agree with this. Even if paid employment is unlikely in some cases to provide autonomous *work* because few find making cardboard boxes or driving buses appealing as major life goals, it can still be made pleasant enough to attract autonomous *agents*. Significant cuts in working hours may, indeed, lead to improvements in both areas just distinguished. Not only would autonomous people be more willing to take on pleasant heteronomous work if it encroached less on their time. Some of them might also be more prepared to see making cardboard boxes as a major personal goal, at least for a period, provided it left them enough time for whatever else they wanted. What is unbearable about present arrangements is the thought that, however socially useful the product I am helping to make, *so much of my life* has to be devoted to this that I have no life of my own. A significant cut in working hours could enable me to think, 'As well as my music, my friends and my love of the countryside, it means a lot to me to be able to do my bit for other people in the wider community. Precisely what I do is not so important: I'll turn a hand to anything.' In other words, helping to make cardboard boxes is not a major goal in itself, but only the concrete filling of a major goal to do with doing one's bit for the community[1]. (An historical parallel is people on 'the home front' making munitions in the Second World War.) Of course, one would have to be confident that what one was producing was indeed beneficial: it might be harder to convince oneself of this if working in a cigarette factory than making crockery. This qualification apart, the more this kind of conceptualisation of otherwise unlikely major goals becomes possible, the nearer Dahrendorf's ideal is approached of transforming jobs into 'activity'.

We are approaching the limits of what philosophy, even in its most practical form as applied ethics, can contribute to future policy on work. As Dahrendorf asks, 'How ... do people earn their living if not in jobs? On what basis are taxes levied? How are the entitlements of social policy determined?' (p 184). We might add: 'How can we equitably distribute jobs and non-paid work? How can we avoid social fracturing into those privileged by cushioned, well-paid jobs on the one hand and those disadvantaged by insecure or no employment on the other? Should there be maxima on the total amount of paid employment one can do in a week, or – following Gorz – in a lifetime?' Like Dahrendorf, I shall not broach issues like these. What is needed before hammering out policies is sufficient agreement about broad directions and the values on which these rest.

DISTRIBUTING WORK

This said, there is just one more philosophically-based thought I would like to add. The biggest practical task ahead concerns distribution. Echoing a widely felt anxiety, William Bridges writes:

> When I was growing up, we used to read that by the year 2000 everyone would have to work only 30 hours a week and that the rest would be leisure time. But as we approach the year 2000, it seems more likely that half of us will work 60 hours a week or longer and the rest of us will be unemployed. What is going wrong?' ('The death of the job' *The Independent on Sunday*, 6 February 1995).

Will Hutton's (1995, pp 105ff) description of the 'thirty, thirty, forty society', divided into 30 per cent economically inactive, 30 per cent in insecure jobs and 40 per cent in privileged, well-paid ones, is a finer-grained analysis, but we can discern beneath both accounts a radically inequitable distribution of goods associated with personal well-being: income, interesting activity, free time, social recognition.

How should work best be distributed? It is hard to know how to answer this in the abstract, given the distinctions that exist among different types of work: paid work, voluntary work, autonomous work, heteronomous work, etc. We also need to know whether we are talking about distributing benefits (as when we talk about the distribution of income or university places), or burdens (as in talk about income tax). Work can be both beneficial and burdensome, partly depending on its general type. Autonomous work is broadly speaking the former; heteronomous work may be one or the other, depending on eg. how much of one's time it takes up, its pleasantness or unpleasantness/dangerousness/boringness, its financial rewards or non-rewards, its high or low status.

We need to target real issues. Some of our categories do not seem to generate these. Suppose we ask how autonomous work should be distributed across the population. What kind of answer might we expect? That everyone should engage in it? But what grounds could there be in a liberal society to insist on this? This looks like, and is, unjustified paternalism. All we can do is to go back to the liberal ideal of autonomous well-being for all and try to arrange things so that more people come closer to achieving this. How they decide to spend their autonomous existence – via what mix of non-work activity, autonomous work and heteronomous work – is up to them, given their circumstances.

Egalitarianism comes into such a social policy only at the abstract level of equal respect for everyone as an autonomous person, where 'respect' covers not only stand-off values of non-interference, but also a positive concern that people have to possess the wherewithal, the necessary conditions of autonomy (adequate income, adequate time to themselves, education, liberty, etc). No more stringent sense of 'equality' is implied than this – that everyone has the same income, for instance, or the same amount of free time. No good reason for such strict equality (or reduction of inequality) has been given to my knowledge, despite many attempts of philosophers convinced that strict equality of income or wealth, educational attainment, well-being, etc is desirable for its own sake (see White 1994b). This kind of egalitarianism is in this way very different from advocating universal equality of respect, since the latter is a value at the core of and inextricably linked with the notion of a liberal democratic society.

The principle of universal equality of respect directs us to helping people to attain the wherewithal for autonomous well-being. Those who are farthest away from the goal require more help, so our efforts should be weighted in their favour. This generates a social policy on say, income, not of providing everyone with an equal amount of money, but of concentrating first on the poorest in an attempt to make them less badly off.

How is all this connected with the distribution of work? Very directly. I have suggested so far that we should not break our heads attaching sense to this notion, but should concentrate on trying to realise the ideal of autonomous well-being for all, leaving it to individuals to decide what place work of different kinds should have in their lives. This points to helping first those most lacking in the necessary conditions of autonomous well-being.

Some of these necessary conditions bring us back to work, especially where it is a burden. We thus return to heteronomous work and its impact on well-being. In a culture like ours where work has become so dominant, many would prefer more time away from it. In addition, some heteronomous work is badly paid, unwantedly dangerous or boring, low in status and recognition, organised on authoritarian lines or insecure.

There are other burdens, too, which deprive people of the necessary conditions of autonomous well-being – non-voluntary unemployment, for instance. As things are today, unemployment often brings with it low income, low public- and therefore self-regard, disorientation and anxiety. Many of these disadvantages are compounded the longer a person is out of work.

Philippe van Parijs (1995) implicitly points to another such burden. His Californian surfer (see above, p 41) does not want a job. But his income as an unemployed person may not be enough to enable him to live for surfing. Van

Parijs argues, as we have seen, for a high basic income for everyone, regardless of whether they are in work or not. He suggests ways in which this basic income can be raised, e.g. by taxing job-holders. For our purposes, his book is helpful in identifying another work-related burden – and one which may become less recondite if 'Californian' values become more widespread as the work-ethic recedes.

A final type of work-related obstacle to autonomous well-being is failing to land the sort of job one would prefer and having to put up with something radically unappealing. Think of someone with a PhD in sociology intent on an academic career, but having to temp so as to make ends meet. If jobs become harder to get, this kind of burden will surely increase.

There are no doubt other kinds of burden than these, but these are enough for present purposes. The kind of egalitarian policy I am suggesting, based on equal respect rather than 'strict equality', enjoins trying to remove the more onerous deficiencies first. This leads to the question: which are the worse burdens?

It may be difficult to adjudicate about the undesirability of, say, a fairly ill-paid unpleasant job in a slaughterhouse for thirty hours a week as against pittance-waged mechanical work in a factory for forty. Apart from other other considerations, people's differing preferences and aversions come too much into the picture. But *some* kind of hierarchy is surely possible. Whatever sympathy I had for the would-be surfer's inability to support his lifestyle, I would want more to be done for victims of sweated labour in the garment industry or for the long-term (non-voluntary) unemployed. The points at which policy pressures should be most urgently applied are fairly clear.

So far, we have looked at types of burden, but not at the accumulation of burdens that can accrue to specific groups. Blacks in Britain are over-represented in low-paid, unattractive, insecure, long-houred jobs as well as among the non-voluntarily unemployed. Working-class women are often also disadvantaged, by unpaid household chores as well as by jobs with multiple drawbacks. Relieving group deprivations of these sorts should be a major policy priority.

As the worst cases are successfully tackled, political attention can turn to lesser evils – the frustrations of those who have to put up with jobs they don't like, for instance – even, in time, those of van Parijs' surfer.

As to how the burdens might be lifted, this is a complex issue and would take us into detailed political and economic argument out of place in this book. But the principle of universal equality of respect can itself be something of a guideline, as Michael Walzer's discussion of 'hard work' (Walzer 1983, ch 6) implicitly shows. Multiple disadvantages can be disaggregated – so that if a person is doing dangerous work, e.g. as a miner or fireman, this should not be aggravated by low pay or long hours. According hard or boring jobs high wages for shorter hours is in line with this version of egalitarianism since it compensates shortfalls from autonomous well-being in one direction with a fuller meeting of its necessary conditions in another.

Some burdens may be deemed so great that they are not compensatable in this way. No one should be expected to work sixty hours a week. No one should be pushed around by callous or manipulating bosses, or have to work with unsafe machinery. Legislation on maximum working hours, on workers' democratic rights and on safety at work may well be necessary.

Other burdens may be alleviated by creating new ranges of possibilities. I am thinking here especially of the growth of the voluntary sector. If a young person cannot get her dream paid job as a countryside ranger, she can work for a year or two as a conservation volunteer. And the more society, as it becomes able to afford this, moves in a van Parijs direction towards a high basic income for every citizen, the larger portion of a lifetime will voluntary work become able to fill.

NOTES

1. Can a conceptual alchemist turn all heteronomous work into autonomous? Activities in which people engage can be conceptualised in an indefinite number of ways. What I am doing at the moment can be variously described as 'typing words', 'using a computer, 'writing a book', 'trying to influence opinion'. If making cardboard boxes or cleaning sewers can be seen also as 'working for the community' or 'helping people to lead fulfilled lives', cannot this work, under such wider descriptions, be seen as realising one's major goals as an autonomous person?

   If so, rather than reducing heteronomous work, should not social policy be directed towards encouraging workers to reconceptualise it in this way?

   I don't think so. This could be a route to tyranny – and has been, in the labour policies of the twentieth century's totalitarian regimes. Putting pressure on factory workers to see themselves, first and foremost, as builders of communism is not to treat them as autonomous persons.

   This said, reconceptualisation can be compatible with autonomy, as in the example of the cardboard box maker in the text.

FOUR

Education and the future of work

INTRODUCTION

How should parents, teachers and educational policy-makers in Britain and comparable countries conceive the relationship between education and work? This is not a question that can be answered in the abstract. If we could see into the future how things will be in 2050 or 2100, we would be better placed. But the future of work is radically uncertain. This is not only because the future in general is unpredictable, but more particularly because we have no guarantee that the combination of technological change and growing scepticism about work's centrality which could herald the coming of 'the activity society' will in fact bring us closer to it. Instead, the work society may still be with us far into the next century. We may not all follow the former Secretary of State for Education, John Patten, in believing that 'we need the help of religious education in order to underpin a re-born theology of work which in its turn can be a foundation for the legitimacy of the free market' (*Times Educational Supplement*, 9 June 1995). But there are enough other signs that the centrality doctrine is far from dead. Over the next decades its disbenefits to individuals' well-being may even grow rather than diminish.

It makes sense, then, to discuss education and work against two possible scenarios – the continuance, or hardening, of the status quo; and its gradual transformation into a society in which heteronomous work is – for everyone – far less dominant.

SCENARIO 1: STATUS QUO

The British government's resistance in the mid-1990s to the European Union's restriction of paid employment under the conditions of the Social Chapter to 48 hours maximum per week reminds us how entrenched traditional attitudes still are. Setting maxima is seen as a threat to industrial efficiency by pushing up labour costs and thus making British firms less able to compete in the global economy, not least against the so-called 'tiger economies' of Eastern Asia with their supplies of cheap labour.

Despite the progress of automation, with all its potentialities for beneficent work-reduction, the shifts in employment patterns it has brought with it in recent years fit neatly into the ideology of work. We are witnessing a new three-way social division of the working population, mirrored in institution after institution across public, private and voluntary sectors, into [a] a growing number of unemployed or otherwise economically inactive people; [b] a periphery of workers, often casual, on short-term contracts or part-time, who can be hired and fired flexibly as employment demands dictate; and [c] a core of better paid full-time and long-serving part-time staff. As we have seen, Will Hutton (1995) describes these three groups, taken together, as 'the thirty, thirty, forty society' after the percentage of the working population found in each respectively. These groups constitute a hierarchy (running now from [c] to [a]), from what Hutton calls 'the privileged' through the 'marginalised and insecure' to the 'disadvantaged.' Putting things in these terms underlines the way traditional attitudes to work are currently being reinforced. For most people the most sought-after state is still a secure, full-time job, with insecure employment at least a preferable alternative to unemployment. 'Full employment', in the sense of full-time work for all, is still a taken-for-granted political ideal across much of the party spectrum, even though hopes of attaining it diminish with the years.

Without deliberate political intervention, current trends look set to continue. In Britain the proportion of full-time, tenured jobs (i.e. those in the privileged category [c]) fell from 55 per cent of the adult population in 1975 to 35 per cent in 1993. With further job-losses through automation, the central core may come to consist largely of managerial and professional staff, thus helping to entrench a society polarised between the rich and powerful few and the rest.

Not surprisingly, competition for a decreasing amount of work has enabled employers to insist on working conditions for their staff favourable to themselves, including long, often increasingly long, working hours. This favours another kind of social polarisation, between those in work, obliged sometimes to take more than one job, who are left with too little time to themselves, and the unemployed who are saddled with too much.

Those in work, securely or insecurely, will need to adapt flexibly to the frequent changes on the work scene caused by market forces and technological innovation as well as by personal factors. The insecure workers in category [b], as well as those of the unemployed who manage to find work, may well have to switch from one job direction to another in order to survive; while the managers and professionals in category [c] will have to command a wide array of skills to respond to the rapid and complex twists of a globalised economy.

On Scenario I the broad framework of the welfare state as we know it will continue to exist as a necessary adjunct to the work society. Any such society, where paid employment is at the centre of social life, will need some kind of provision for those outside the economic system – the unemployed and the pensioners. There will be room within the framework for political differences about the extent and sources of such provision, but the framework itself will be taken as read.

Educational reactions

The future is unpredictable; and the patterns which seem now to be crystallising may turn out otherwise. But if the future of work is indeed along these lines, how will educators and policy-makers respond?

They will continue to give young people an orientation towards their life in which paid employment is its central preoccupation – whether or not they succeed in securing it. People will be brought up to define the different stages of their life in relation to this centrality. Their childhood will be partly a period of insulation from the world of work and partly a preparation for some kind of role within that world. The core of their existence will remain their adult life up to retiring age: whether they are in work or out, and whether any work they have is secure or insecure, work will still be at the centre of their activities or thoughts. When they are unemployed, it is their thoughts which will be all-important – thoughts embodied in their self-identification as 'unemployed', with further work-related thoughts embedded in the emotions of shame, low self-respect and envy which so many of them will be likely to feel. The third period of their lives will be their retirement – or, if they have had no work from which to retire, their years as pensioners. So, from the point of view of young people looking ahead along the time line of their lives, at every point a large part of their self-definition will be internally connected to paid employment.

One specific way in which educators and policy-makers can prepare the young for a work-dominated life will be by helping them to be as well equipped as possible to occupy some role or other within the newly stratifying society. This could mean equipping the abler among them with the advanced skills and competitive drive necessary for entry into the privileged, core group; and giving the rest more basic skills, together with positive dispositions towards new skill-learning and coping with job insecurity, that living inside category [b] brings with it. If long-term unemployment increases, perhaps in local or regional pockets, 'education for unemployment' may even become a fixed part of the vocational landscape. (In 1996 it already exists in a small way on deprived estates in north-east England.)

This kind of pattern is compatible with all kinds of more specific arrangements. Politically, both left and right could adapt to it. It could go with a selective educational system, with pupils divided at an early age into those attending schools likely to see them into category [c] employment and the rest. It could also go with the comprehensive ideal of keeping all children in the same school throughout. This would give more children the chance to stay longer in the competition for attractive vocational destinations.

Schools have not by any means seen their aims as wholly vocational. They prepare pupils for life, not just for work. The [a]-[b]-[c] pattern is compatible not only with widely different *institutional* arrangements, but also with different reactions to the traditional *curricular* split between liberal and vocational studies. On the one hand the division between these two could be maintained. British post-sixteen education could still embrace both students taking the academic, A-level route, ostensibly for liberal reasons to do with learning for its own sake or in order to broaden their cultural horizons, but also at least in part to maximise their higher education and later job opportunities; and those taking vocational, e.g. GNVQ, courses. On the other hand, liberal/academic and vocational orientations could be merged together in an undifferentiated sixth-form – and possibly post-18 – system. Current policy reforms – e.g. the Dearing post-16 recommendations – as well as academic challenges to the liberal-vocational divide (e.g. R Pring 1995, especially ch 8) are all urging us towards a unified system, although how strong traditional resistance proves remains to be seen.

If the regime of work continues in its new [a]-[b]-[c] form, we are likely to see continued tussles over selection versus non-selection and over divided versus unified curricula. These may well form a large part of the political agenda. One effect of this might be to turn attention *inwards*, that is, to what divides the policy-makers, and away from the [a]-[b]-[c] framework they all take for granted. The more fundamental issue, about whether this framework is acceptable, may become submerged.

This would be regrettable, because, for reasons fully spelt out earlier in this book, the regime of work needs to be transcended, not shored-up. The new [a]-[b]-[c] society is ethically unacceptable on several counts. It polarises prospects of well-being, with income, security of employment and quality of work experience flowing towards the privileged and leaving large parts of the population disadvantaged. It perpetuates the traditional doctrine of the centrality of work, shown in these pages and elsewhere to be intellectually unfounded. Indeed, this centrality is likely to be strengthened further in the [a]-[b]-[c] society, as struggles for the less work there is around intensify and as long working hours are taken as read.

Many teachers will not want to help perpetuate such a system. They will not want to see themselves as agents of salvation for the more fortunate or agents of insecurity for the rest. They have become teachers for nobler reasons – to liberate young minds, to help all their charges to lead fulfilling lives. They are right to hold fast to these ideals.

Unfortunately, if present trends continue, such idealism may itself be increasingly eroded. I have in mind partly the effects of the [a]-[b]-[c] revolution on the teaching force itself. If schools follow the pattern of other institutions and come to comprise a privileged, tenured core staff and a penumbra of teachers on short-term contracts, too many of the latter will be preoccupied with their own job security to luxuriate in thoughts about how things might be different. A second dampener of idealism has already been with us for several years in the shape of the reorganisation of teacher education. Teachers' noses have been kept close to the classroom grindstone, with little encouragement to think about wider educational issues: the role of universities in initial teacher education has been reduced and funds for non-nitty-gritty inservice education have been slashed. In addition the National Curriculum has reinforced the conception of teachers as subject-specialists. It has directed their attention inwards on to the details of prescribed objectives in their area and away, once again, from the larger issues.

Despite these current tendencies, teachers should do all they can to hold on to a more generous conception of their task. Even if employment policy in general hardens along [a]-[b]-[c] lines, schools could use the curricular freedom left to them to encourage pupils to think not only about their own futures within this framework but also about the ethical acceptability of the framework itself. Need things be as they are? Need life be such a struggle for survival? Are there better ways of arranging society than in such a hierarchy of well-being? If work is scarce, are there not ways of sharing it out, to most people's advantage? Need work so dominate our picture of a flourishing life?

Some readers of the *Daily Telegraph* will bridle at this suggestion that teachers should urge pupils to think about fundamental social questions. 'We had enough of this kind of revolutionary activity in the sixties and seventies. The conservative reforms of the last seventeen years have done away with most of it, redirecting teachers' attention on to their proper, classroom, tasks and away from such subversion. The coming of the National Curriculum has made it clear that the content of education is for the state, and behind the state, for parents, to decide. Teachers are executives of others' decisions. Legitimate scope for their own, autonomous input comes only at the level of effective teaching. The broad framework should rightly be left to political, not professional control.'

Having myself argued for nearly three decades that the state should fix the aims and broad content of school curricula, I have some sympathy with this last comment. But only *some* sympathy. In an ideal world, the broader framework of the curriculum should not be determined by a section of the population – i.e. by teachers – but by the citizenry as a whole. Just as, in a democratic society, we would not think of leaving military policy in the hands of generals, or taxation policy in the hands of tax inspectors, neither should we brook leaving education policy to teachers. Matters like all these, which affect the global contours and well-being of our society, should be the province of the democracy as a whole. All this is true. But it is true only at the level of political ideals. The actual democratic society in which we live only imperfectly reflects democratic principles, not least the fundamental principle that every member of the democracy is equal in intrinsic importance to every other member and has an

equal moral right to the conditions of a flourishing life. Condoning and promoting the [a]-[b]-[c] society when policy decisions could have gone in quite
another direction offends against this principle.

Just as teachers would be released from their prima facie restriction to a
merely executive role if, say, a national government organised school curricula
on racist lines, so they are similarly absolved if debarred from questioning a
deeply questionable employment policy. More generally, if it is accepted that
democratic citizens need, as political decision-makers, some broad understanding of central political issues, a system which refuses them this needs to
be challenged in the name of democracy itself. Teachers have every right – and
every responsibility – to help their pupils towards this understanding.

SCENARIO 2: BEYOND THE WORK SOCIETY

The first scenario of future possibilities was that heteronomous work will
retain its central place in the culture. The second is that the centrality doctrine
will come under growing challenge as we move into a society premised on a
more liberal view of human well-being.

In 1996, the year in which I write, there are many signs that the challenge is
already under way. The European Union has legislated a maximum working
week of 48 hours; and although the current British government has opted out
of this, there is wide electoral support for it. Forty-eight hours is a long week,
of course, and does not in itself challenge the centrality ideology; but once the
principle of legislated maxima is accepted, the way lies open to their progressive reduction.

More significant, perhaps, is the growing awareness of the imbalances and
injustices of the status quo, polarised as it is between people working harder
than ever and people with not enough work, and with wealth and power arro-
gated increasingly to a privileged core. 'The future of work' is now a staple
topic in the quality press – not only *The Independent* – scarcely a week passing
without lengthy articles on 'The death of the job' or 'Whatever happened to
nine to five?' Publishers, too, find a ready market for books like Jeremy Rifkin's
(1995) *The End of Work*. Not only authors and journalists make the running.
Under the headline 'Britons tire of consumerism' a MORI poll in 1995 found
that over the last quarter of a century the proportion of people 'rejecting
materialism and 'conspicuous consumption' in favour of personal fulfilment
and quality of life' had gone up from 5 per cent to 20 per cent. For the first
time, these 'post-materialists' had come to outnumber those who attach a high
value to economic issues (15 per cent) (*The Independent*, 4 June 1995).

Britain seems on the brink of a more general cultural shift, embracing not
only beliefs towards work and consumption, but also attitudes to religion,
morality, the family, the monarchy, nationality, the constitution. In sphere after
sphere traditional responses are under threat, in some cases perhaps even mor-
tal threat. It is hard to remember a time when so much of the social framework

was simultaneously under such intense scrutiny. And since these cultural gird-ers all interlock, the doctrine of work, for instance, having, as we have seen, close historical connexions with religious ideas and the obligation-centred tenets of traditional morality, it is likely that underminings in one area will has-ten them in another.

If work patterns do change, the conventional picture of a flourishing life as built around a lifetime, full-time job will yield to more liberal and more pluralistic conceptions. A life of self-chosen activities will become the new cul-tural ideal. How work should figure in it will be less monolithic. Most people will want to spend part of their time in paid employment, especially if working conditions become more person-centred or democratically arranged; most, again, will prefer plenty of free time to get on with other things, while some are likely to find fulfilment in a more conventional career. Voluntary work – Rifkin's 'third sector' – should become an attractive option for many of those with more time off from a paid job, and for some of those – the young, the retired, the unemployed – who have no paid job at all. Autonomous work of other sorts – creative, scholarly, practical – may also be expected to blossom; as may autonomous activities which have nothing to do with work – sports, social-ising, enjoying works of art.

What place will there be for heteronomous work within the new order? There is no question, this side of Utopia, of its complete disappearance. Leaving aside its more attractive forms, that is, those accommodatable to the requirements of autonomous agency, in any society there will be unpleasant work which people would not do by choice. Will this matter? Not necessarily. Provided trade-offs are favourable enough, some will be willing to use financial and other benefits attached to it to support, for example, their expensive pref-erences as autonomous agents. The requirement of universal autonomy would also rule out the tendency found in most societies, including our own, of unpleasant work's being associated with particular social groups or with an 'underclass'. No one should be fated to spend their one life so intolerably. Rewards – not only financial – for unpleasant work should be high enough to attract autonomous individuals from any walk of life willing to accept the trade-off.

There is another way in which unpleasant work may become conceptu-alised. The autonomous agents we are envisaging are not egoists, but socially responsive persons. For some of them their altruistic needs will be fulfilled in activities which are fully autonomous in that they embody major intrinsic pref-erences – by work as a teacher, for instance, or through the interactions of friendship. Others will want to do more. Voluntary workers today find them-selves manning tills in charity shops. This is not unpleasant like mining coal or working in a slaughterhouse, but – from one perspective, at least – it is not autonomous work. Operating a till is not likely to be an intrinsically significant major option in anyone's life. Once, however, it is reconceptualised, not *just* as manning a till, but as 'working for Oxfam' or 'helping to bring about a cure for

cancer', it is easy to see how it can become something of great personal significance in someone's life. This happens, of course, already and on an increasing
scale. Could we not imagine the same happening to unpleasant work? Its really objectionable feature is the central place it has in some unfortunate people's
lives. But in the post-productivist society there may well be some people willing to undertake it as an autonomous choice in the reconceptualised way
described – at least for a few hours a week or for a part of their lives. If there is
more unpleasant work to be done than can be met either by the altruism just
referred to or the trade-offs mentioned earlier, some kind of compulsory community service for everyone seems the answer most consonant with the ideal of
universal autonomy. Spread across the population, its burdens should encroach
minimally on the autonomy ideal.

In the post-productivist scenario ethical attitudes towards paid work will
also change. It will no longer be a universal obligation, with its cruel corollary
that those out of a job fall morally short. The 'virtue' of industriousness, in the
shape of willingness to work hard at a job however uncongenial it might be, will
be dethroned. Nietzsche's reassessment (see page 40 above) will become the
new conventional wisdom. While people would still be praised for the hard
work they put into autonomous work activities, this would not be a moral judgment, carrying with it the thought that they are only doing what they ought to
do, but more a celebration of a human fulfilment. 'Work-shy' will become a
term looking for employment. 'Idleness' will no longer be a state to be
deplored. Human beings being what they are, we could count on a loosening-
up of the work regime to lead to their filling their free time with activities of all
kinds. Might some people be 'activity-shy'? 'Activity-shyness' is something
hard for us to conceive. The only sense we can attach to it is pathological: the
torpor of the depressed or ill.

These ethical changes, as well as the new order of work/activity, have implications for educational policy, as we shall see. So do other cultural shifts probably consequent on these changes. Class/status divisions are unlikely to stay
unaffected. At present these are closely tied to the work order, high social status – the very rich apart – being a function of a professional or managerial job
with all the life-benefits this brings. The diminished salience of 'the job' in
individuals' lives should help to flatten status hierarchies. And also to redis-
tribute social recognition (that often underestimated condition of well-being)
away from wealth, power, conventional success and towards the broader range
of achievements and personal qualities encouraged in the activity society.
Gender and ethnic differences will also be affected. Despite equal opportunity
legislation, the difficulties some women and non-English employees have in
landing the more desirable jobs are well-known. While removing these obstacles would still be a major priority, a shift away from productivism can also be
relied on to alleviate the problem. As with status, I do not mean to be over-
optimistic here: older attitudes are hard to shift. Even so, a gradual – and perhaps not so gradual – opening-up of wider perspectives on what makes a

human life worth living is now very much on the cards.

Still on gender, any dilution of the work culture is bound to bring with it a softening of the edges between traditional masculine and feminine perspectives on life. The work-society has been built around a duality: a man's fate has been a life of paid labour, a woman's, home and children. The former has been built around instrumental values – activities orientated towards the production of goods and services from the enterprise's point of view, a wage-packet from the individual's. More person-centred and emotion-involving concerns have traditionally been split off from this masculine world and left to women. Throughout the twentieth century these rigidities have eased to some extent with the entry of more and more women into the labour force and the successes of the women's movement with its critique of the centrality of masculine values and its call for an ethics of care to be spread more universally across the population. As Scenario 2 becomes more salient, we can expect the balance to tip even more towards human-centred values. Men's and women's lives will become more alike. More central to both will be self-chosen and fulfilling activities, including paid employment, but not dominated by it. The pattern will vary from individual to individual, with men and women sharing domestic activities much more than in the past. At home and outside, for both sexes the central ethical values will revolve around personal autonomy and concern for the flourishing of those around one. Intimacy and friendship, in particular, can be expected to move more centre-stage – along with that greater reflectiveness about one's life and one's relationships associated, once again, with traditional feminine attitudes.

Scenario 2 will make us more alike – but not in any sense that should disturb or call up Orwellian images of unbearable uniformity. We will be more alike only in that for each of us the ideal picture we have of our lives will be of largely self-chosen, personally fulfilling and socially beneficial activities. Men will be guided by this picture, as will be women. Children will be initiated into it. Older people will follow it as much as younger, the sharp lines separating one's 'productive' life from 'retirement' becoming less and less relevant. It will mean as much to the less affluent – provided they have *enough* resources – as to the rich: the latter's range of options may be wider, but a fulfilling life should be within the reach of all, or nearly all, of us. Although society will become more alike in this way across its traditional fracture-lines, in another way it will be more variegated. This follows, indeed, from the type of uniformity in question: in a self-directing society, patterns of individuals' lives – the threads of activities which constitute them – are likely to differ one from another more than in a society where work's exigencies determine so much.

This completes the sketch of Scenario 2. It is not a utopian vision. It does not envisage a dramatic rejection of the work culture, an imminent transition to a hippy paradise or communist society in which what work there is is all autonomous. Realistically, the total of heteronomous work can be reduced, or reapportioned, only gradually. But even five or six hours cut from the standard

British working week could herald the end of work's dominance in our lives. Depending on the individual, there must be some point along the scale of a shorter and shorter working week at which work becomes of secondary rather than primary importance to one, and for many thirty to thirty-five hours may be approaching this. According to some analysts, more dramatic reductions are on the horizon over the next couple of decades (Rifkin 1995). It is too simple, of course, to limit changes to work-reduction of this sort, to paid and largely heteronomous employment. The likely growth of voluntary work and the increased opportunities for other kinds of autonomous work and autonomous non-work activities could complicate things kaleidoscopically, helping to bring about that growing – and gradual – variegation in individuals' life-patterns of work and non-work activity which we encountered above.

EDUCATION FOR THE ACTIVITY SOCIETY

With some exceptions, children born in the year 2000 will live through most of the twenty-first century. On our second scenario, they may spend the best part of their adult lives in a society where work no longer dominates, but where different kinds of work – paid, unpaid/voluntary, heteronomous, autonomous, part-time, full-time, tenured, casual – are woven into fuller patterns of self-chosen activities.

What changes in the way we think about education would this bring with it?

First, a qualification. Putting things in terms of two contrasting scenarios may seem to leave the role of education merely reactive, on the lines of: if Scenario 1 comes about, its task would be this; if Scenario 2, that. But education can help to create social futures as well as reflect them. If, as has been argued in this book, Scenario 2 is ethically preferable to Scenario 1, its virtues should be made apparent to young people – who should not be brought up under the illusion that Scenario 1 is all that there could be. I am not advocating indoctrinating them into a preference for 2, only bringing it home to them first as a possibility and second as a possibility which has serious arguments in favour of it: as autonomous beings in the making, they must make up their own minds how far they go along with it. At all events, the acceptability of the work culture being as controversial as it now is, there is no reason why the education system should any longer take it as read. This might not count as indoctrination in a strict sense of the term, since there cannot be many teachers around who consciously aim at inculcating attachment to the work culture and preventing their pupils from reflecting on it. But on a broader interpretation, institutional arrangements can be indoctrinatory even if individuals working within them have no such intentions: an educational system premised on hard work as a child in preparation for hard work as an adult may still have the effect of implanting the doctrine of work in children's minds and discouraging doubt about it. Whatever the terminology we prefer, at least educators have good reasons for softpedalling children's traditional socialisation into work-mindedness so as to let them see work in its different forms against wider horizons of well-being.

With this qualification in mind, let us come back to Scenario 2. How should education be reconceptualised on the assumption that the next century will see its coming – perhaps spurred on by educational activities themselves, as well as by technological changes and political decisions?

I shall be assuming in what follows that education goes beyond schooling or other kinds of formal preparation. Education is basically upbringing. It starts in the home with parents as the child's first educators. School education continues the parents' work, extending it into areas beyond which they are equipped, or have the time, to cope. So do post-school educational institutions like universities and adult education colleges. The culture in which children grow up is also an educative force, helping insensibly to shape attitudes and behaviour by the taken-for-grantedness of its institutions. (In mainstream British culture, but not in some others, children grow up never doubting that, if they marry, they will freely choose their spouse, or that if they have the money they can live in whatever part of the country they like.)

We shall need to look individually at how each of these educators – families, schools, post-school institutions, the culture – can help to prepare young people for Scenario 2. But before we tackle this – which essentially concerns *procedures* – we need to broach logically prior questions about *objectives*. What should the educators just mentioned be aiming at?

The educational impact of the culture

A word, first, about the educational impact of the culture. It may seem odd to include the culture along with the other agencies just mentioned as an 'educator' where this is taken to imply aim-directedness. Cultures, it may be said, can certainly *influence* individuals, and for that reason may properly be called, as they were called above, 'educative forces'; but all this happens non-deliberately, without the conscious aim of bringing about learning of different kinds found among parents and school teachers.

While it is probably generally true that cultural shaping has in the past been the unconscious product of tradition, this does not mean that it always has to be. In our own highly reflective age, things can be and are very different. Our *modi operandi* in different spheres of our social life involve traditions, but are not for the most part tradition-directed. Typically they face the challenges of rational justification and typically they have ways of answering the challenges – ways not always universally compelling, but at least opening the way to further dialogue. All this means that cultural phenomena are no longer given, but can be consciously set new directions. Traditional beliefs and practices about the roles of men and women provide a particularly clear example from the last two or three decades. Of course, culture-reformers by no means always have educational aims in mind. The women's movement has wanted among other things greater equality between the sexes at work, the ecologists a less polluted planet, etc. But education can be, and often is, *one* of the aims powering such movements. Feminists have set out to change people's beliefs about gender-roles, to heighten their reflectiveness about their emotional reactions. There are countless other examples from other social causes.

It still may seem odd to talk of 'the culture' as an aim-orientated educator. Should we not say it is the culture-reformers – the feminists, conservationists, health-promoters, innovative artists, broadcasters like Lord Reith, humanists, etc – who are the educators, and not anything so impersonal and amorphous as the culture itself? I have no problem with this, as long as the non-intended educative influence of culture is also recognised. In fact, pinpointing culture-reformers in this way places them clearly in the same category as other educators like parents and school teachers – as *persons* involved in educating and therefore as persons who need to reflect on their aims and how best to realise them. Their work is often not confinable to easily defined social roles like that of parent or teacher. It is also ranged along a continuum from full-time activists wholly concerned with education at one end through to part-time volunteers mainly working towards other social objectives, but involved in consciousness-raising to a minor extent. Even putting things like this risks underestimating the – almost certainly growing – number of people caught up in educational work, or potentially educational work. Many enterprises have staff appraisal schemes, codes of practice about sexual harassment, equal opportunities for the disabled, policies on non-smoking. There are innumerable ways in which staff involved in these practices can consciously try, in smaller or larger ways, to change colleagues' perceptions. Some may go too far in a paternalist direction; but there is plenty of evidence today of benigner forms of ethos-shaping.

We have broadened the focus well beyond culture-reformers in any usual sense. Now that we have done so, another question arises. Do educators at work in the culture at large include only those who seek to *change* perceptions and beliefs? Whether we take social campaigners like feminist activists or people upholding ethical codes on a day-to-day basis within enterprises, it would be wrong to see all the people whom they seek to influence as *falling short* in their perceptions etc. Where consciousness-raising is the target, some falling-short, or at least some assumption of falling-short, *does* seem to be implied. But part of the work of cultural educators in different parts of our spectrum has to do with *reinforcing* perceptions which people already possess. If this is admissible as a form of educating, it is applicable even more widely than to the people mentioned so far. When I thank a stranger for some small favour, I can do it in such a way as to make him feel good about himself – and I can consistently give people recognition of this and other sorts, guided dispositionally by the at-some-point-conscious thought that reinforcing other people's favourable conceptions of themselves, where appropriate, is a civilised thing to do. In a highly reflective age like our own, many of us are cultural educators in a small way most days of our lives. At some point consciously-directed activity of this sort shades into less reflective forms of reinforcement typical of a more tradition-directed society and still massively present in a society like our own. When we use the language of 'please' and 'thank you' not all of us, by any means, link what we do with larger thoughts about helping to cement civilised attitudes. We come back at this point to the notion, discussed above, of the educative influence that the culture can have on individuals even though no one has such influencing consciously in mind.

To come back to our main topic. I was making a distinction between the aims of education in a post-productivist society and the types of educators who could help to realise them. Having sorted out a problem about the latter, we can now concentrate on the former.

Aims of education in a post-productivist society

What aims should guide educators if we are indeed moving towards Scenario 2? How far should their aims change from those more fitting for a work culture?

There is an enormous amount that could be said, and has been said, about what educational aims should be. It would be inappropriate to turn this all over here. At the same time, I'm assuming that a mere list of aims, plucked from the air and reflecting only the writer's subjective preferences, will be of no use to anyone. There needs to be an argued case. To keep things in bounds, wherever appropriate I will abbreviate arguments which can be found in fuller form elsewhere and provide suitable references.

Any account of educational aims must begin with education itself. What we take education to be will clearly help to determine what we think should be its aims. 'Education' is often shorthand for 'formal education' – for what goes in in schools and colleges – but I shall not be using the word in this way here. Neither will I be guided by any stipulative definition of the term which writes certain preferred aims into it, like R S Peters' well-known account of it as initiation into intrinsically worthwhile activities. This last notion skews things from the start towards a learning-for-its-own-sake view of education which unduly narrows perspectives.

Education as upbringing

To keep horizons broad, I shall treat 'education' as broadly synonymous with 'upbringing', leaving it open at this point in what directions upbringing should proceed. This puts the spotlight on the child, including the very young child. It also treats the child as a psychological totality, not giving preference, as many accounts of education do, to intellectual development, but bearing in mind that bringing up children is also a matter of shaping their emotions and wants in desirable directions.

The upbringing approach to the topic has the merit of underscoring the crucial role of parents and families in a child's education. Education starts on Day One of a child's life, perhaps even before this if some accounts of what parents can do for a child in the womb can be believed. Parents are the child's first and main educators. Nursery teachers and school teachers come later, continuing the work of upbringing, ideally in consonance with what parents are doing so as to avoid harmful conflicting messages. I say 'harmful' here, since conflicts of belief and value are endemic to any human being's life and learning to cope with them is a vital part of growing up. The mere fact of conflicts between home and school is nothing in itself to cause alarm, provided always that someone helps children, if they need help, to handle them. But sometimes what schools do is so at odds with what families do, and so without mechanisms in place to rectify this, that children's upbringing can be badly affected.

On this view of education as upbringing, home becomes more salient than school. School education has to fit into the wider framework of upbringing, and here parents and families are key. This reverses how many of us are used to thinking about education in our own society, where the early years are sometimes seen as laying the foundation for the more serious work of education that starts when the child crosses the primary school's threshold. It has implications, as we shall see in more detail later on, for the content of school education, calling for a far more person-centred curriculum than schools have traditionally had. It means the demise of the subject-centred tradition, which in Britain reached its apotheosis with the introduction of the National Curriculum in 1988. Here the lack of fit with home education is maximal, especially for those families with no tradition of academic schooling. Since the National Curriculum came into force, ways have been proposed to bring the two agencies closer together: home-school contracts, for instance, or compulsory homework for primary children. As these stand, they strengthen the primacy of schooling, putting pressures on parents to adjust to schools' demands. The upbringing view of education would reverse priorities.

As we move further into a post-productivist society, the centrality of the home is likely to become more apparent. Schools as we know them are tied into a productivist culture. As they change to fit the new age, person-centred objectives will gradually take over from work-centred ones. In this way school education will mesh more closely in with wider, upbringing, aims. Home will become more important because more people will probably be spending more of their time there than at offices and factories. If we add to this the likely increased use of the home as a base for earning a living which the PC is already ushering in, this trend will grow further.

Political policies on education in Britain are in one way already reflecting the primacy of families. Across the political spectrum the market conception of consumer power has taken hold, with much more emphasis than hitherto – at least at the level of manifestos – on meeting parental preferences in the choice of schools in the light of now publicly available performance data.

Yet the primacy of families which goes with the 'upbringing' conception of education is very different from this market view. The latter is still centred on schooling. When politicians say that parents and not teachers or the state should have the major say in determining their child's education, what they have in mind is their power to influence what school the child will go to. *This* version of family primacy still puts school at the heart of education – unlike the 'upbringing' conception which shifts the focus to the family. The market notion belongs with the notion of the work-society: what is *really* central, for the most part, is not schooling itself but what schooling leads on to – and in the way we have traditionally thought about this, this is 'the world of work'.

We have talked about families and we have talked about schools. I hope it will be reasonably clear how we can see the task of both agencies as upbringing. Can other formal educational institutions – universities, for example – also be viewed as upbringers? Of course, universities teach students of all ages, and one may want to say that if they are in the business of upbringing at all, this can only be with the very youngest of their charges. Even here, there is room for reservations: an eighteen-year-old studying to be a doctor may well have come to college for a professional training, not to help her round off the process of growing up.

I will leave this issue unresolved for the moment. More challenging to the logical framework I have been using is the cultural educator described above (p 80). Am I really claiming that the feminists, upholders of professional ethical codes and more everyday bestowers of social recognition who came into our story just now are agents of *upbringing*? Surely the latter is applicable only to young people, not to the population at large?

I'm not so sure. When we talk about the upbringing of children, we imply some end-state when upbringing is accomplished. A child of seven is still in the process of being brought up; a 'well-brought-up' twenty-five year old is one whose upbringing is complete. Of course, there is no sharp line at the end of the process, no finishing line that the twenty-five-year-old has now crossed. What we mean, broadly speaking, is that she is now a civilised member of the community. She has assimilated the ethical attitudes which being civilised entails. She is now a considerate, self-confident, self-controlled, judicious (etc) person. The temper-tantrums which marked her early adolescence are now well behind her; the kicking over the traces which came a few years later has now been superseded by a more productive tension between autonomy and concern for others.

An unanswered, almost unasked, question these days is: what counts as being 'well brought up'? The account just given provides a small part of the story and, I take it, would be pretty uncontentious. How might the story be developed further? What other kinds of virtue or capability might be included? How far can we proceed without leaving the sphere of uncontentiousness? A particular difficulty facing the British is that 'being well brought up' is a notion hard to disassociate from social status: as often used, it can suggest having acquired certain dispositions traditionally associated with the middle class – e.g. a willingness to fit into the status quo, an absence of radicalism, a British self-deprecatingness or understatement, etc. This is a pity. We badly need to detach the notion of an adequate upbringing from these kinds of historical impedimenta. Working it out in some detail is a necessary preface to any sensible policy on education. Unless we have a clearer idea than we have at present of what the state of being educated – that is, being well brought up – should consist in, we have no rational way of sorting out what procedures we should best employ.

How does all this link up with the problem of the cultural educator? In this way. 'Being well brought up', as we are now interpreting this, is an ideal state which we hope most people will attain, but from which, realistically, we know some people will fall short and perhaps continue to fall short throughout much or all of their adult life. This puts things a little too starkly. The social world is not divided between those who have come up to the mark and those who have not. Richard Peters, in his writings and teachings in philosophy of education, was fond of referring to 'the thin crust of civilisation'. Part of this thinness dwells in ourselves. We all know very well how fragile is our self-confidence, our benevolence, our sense of justice, our even-temperedness: radically alter our economic circumstances or state of health or mood and these virtues may evaporate. We need to be vigilant on their behalf, to keep them bolstered against adversity.

Cultural educators target those who fall short from civilised standards. They also help to *reinforce* them where the crust gets thin. Thus, feminists aim at giving women who need it the self-confidence to cope in a man's world or getting men who need it to be more respectful and considerate of women. A nurse coming to work in a rather acrimonious old people's home may deliberately encourage the mutual giving of social recognition since this is in jeopardy. Both these and others may also deal in reinforcement where this is called for: the mutually-supportive all-women groups which feminists favour can be as much concerned with consciousness-maintaining as with consciousness-raising.

This kind of activity is educational even though it need have nothing to do with the upbringing of young people. What it has in common with the latter is that it helps people to acquire or strengthen civilised forms of thought and behaviour. If one thinks of 'upbringing' less as rearing the young than as bringing people of whatever age – usually the young, since all the young need this, but not only these – up to certain standards, this may make the notion of education I am proposing easier to accept.

On this view education is sometimes of adults, but 'adult education' as we usually understand this is different. The courses which adults do in the history of gardening or remedial English proceed from their self-directed career and leisure choices. They have nothing necessarily to do with bringing them up to civilised standards. They are called 'educational' because of the deep-rooted association in our culture between education and formal forms of learning.

One last point. The more usual idea of adult education is patently non-paternalist. As just stated, people choose courses which fit in with their own preferences. But what shall we say of the consciousness-raisers and other chivviers I have been calling 'cultural educators'? Where people are no longer children, have they not got the right not to be admonished and prodded along by activists of one stripe or another who want to impose their own idiosyncratic beliefs on others?

If the beliefs are indeed idiosyncratic, I think they are on firm ground to object. But not all consciousness-moulders are on a par with bible-clutching sectists who press suburban doorbells. Whether we should all accept the Second Coming is one thing; whether we should all refrain from disadvantaging people on account of their sex or skin colour, another. The second of these is something everyone in a civilised society ought to adhere to, even if not all do so. Where there are serious shortfalls, tied in perhaps, as sexism and racism are, to powerful social structures, a society aspiring to be civilised needs some way of putting pressure on people to come closer to the mark. This is not in itself paternalist, if we imply by this term that there is some kind of illegitimate shaping of other people's thinking in accordance with the shaper's own values. Anti-discrimination is not just the activist's ideal. In a decent society – assuming it is pursued undogmatically and is duly balanced against other values – it should be everybody's.

CLARIFYING EDUCATIONAL AIMS

I said above that we could not get far in determining the aims of education in a post-productivist society without being clear, first of all, what we were going to call 'education'. I hope this requirement has now been adequately addressed. Discovering what the aims of education should be is tantamount to working out what it is to be well brought up.

I'm aware that this may still seem hard to accept. It appears to put all the emphasis on behaviour rather than intellectual learning – almost as if I were trying to revivify some antiquated, public-school version of education as character-formation, or even some finishing-school variant, to do with turning out well-brought up young persons. I want to detach myself from these connotations, at least most of them. The primacy of character-formation is something I can willingly embrace, but I have no brief for the Christian and/or upper-class understandings of this that come out of British history. Moreover – and this brings us to the main charge – I see no reason why character-aims need be incompatible with intellectual ones.

Not only this. Character-, or person-centred-, aims bring knowledge-aims logically with them. This is true whatever view of the well-brought-up person is taken as the ideal. The well-bred conformist has to *know* his or her social conventions. Build some sort of altruism into your model and you commit yourself to fostering the psychological understanding of people's desires and emotions which this necessitates.

We can also turn the whole argument around. If someone wants to make knowledge-aims the heart of education (as so many do), we can press them for their reasons. Answers could come from several directions: [1] the acquisition or pursuit of knowledge and understanding is important for its own sake. No further reasons are required. *Comment*: Why is it important for its own sake? Some people have scholarly predilections, but, assuming that we are dealing with education for all, why should we think that everyone should be inclined that way? After all, there are just so many varied kinds of activity out there to be pursued, from allotment-tending through to xylophone-playing. Why privilege academic pursuits? [2] To survive in world markets we need a workforce with a good general knowledge, not least in science and technology. *Comment*: This may well be true, but is preparation for work what education is centrally about? If education is preparation for life and life revolves around work as the productivist tradition has held, one can see how a case may be fleshed out. But if the doctrine of work's centrality is more than dodgy, this second answer is incomplete. [3] Children need to learn history, science, geography to help them understand the world they live in. They'll need this understanding as a basis of any form of fulfilling life. *Comment*: Now you're talking!

Intellectual aims are important, but not all-important. They must find their due place in a wider conspectus.

Let us recentre on the person – if you like, the 'whole person' of child-centred educational theory. What is our ideal well-brought-up man or woman going to be like? This is the fundamental question. It is where all educational policy-making needs to start – and never does.

A relatively uncontroversial claim is that education has to do with bringing people up to lead good lives. But what is it to lead a good life? The term brings with it, for most of us, two apparently very different connotations. One finger-post points towards altruism, good works and Mother Teresa, the other to personal fulfilment, living the life one wants and Felicity Kendal[1]. Both elements have a place in our ideal, although whether the two are as distinct as we often think is an open question at this stage.

Moral education and beyond

What the other-orientated aspect of the ideal should embrace is in one way reasonably uncontentious, at least in a liberal society like our own. Most of us would agree that it would be good if people were brought up to be truthful, respectful of others' persons, property and privacy, friendly, fair-minded, possessing a sense of humour, concerned for the well-being not only of those close to them, but also of others personally unknown to them in the national community and in other parts of the world. There is a longer list of these and other qualities on which there would be wide consensus.

Where there would be less agreement is on how these qualities are to be characterised and on priorities among them. The productivist age from which we now appear to be emerging has typically thought about these matters in terms of 'morality'. There are moral rules which all are expected to follow, e.g. injunctions against breaking promises, lying, unfairness, physical harm, murder, theft, infringements on personal liberty. Most of these are negative, descendants – for many people these days in a secular form – of the 'Thou shalt nots' of the decalogue and the Christian tradition. Yet no moral code consists wholly of negative duties. The 'Love thy neighbour as thyself' of the Christian heritage tells us what we must actively do, not refrain from doing. This is where controversy tends to begin. What is the scope of this moral duty? Some few try to follow it more strenuously, most are more relaxed. Those at the muscular end of the range bend their whole lives to the service of others, perhaps on the scale of humanity as a whole. Those at the other restrict themselves to more immediate duties to friends and family, plus any help they are able to give to strangers they meet who trip over in the street or fall into canals. As these people see things, the best way they can help others is for the most part by letting them be to lead their own lives, that is, by scrupulously following the 'Thou shalt nots'.

This 'moral' way of characterising the other-orientated side of living well predates the age of productivism but has fitted it hand in glove. What qualities are needed in a population whose life revolves around paid work? Since the latter is built on contracts of employment, one would expect children's moral education to be especially insistent on keeping one's promises. Occupational promises have tended to bring more specific duties in their train – to be punctual, industrious, honest, respectful of property, obedient to authority. At work and outside people have been expected to be sober, peaceable, law-abiding. There has been no need to extend their positive morality beyond the minimum end of the spectrum: from a commercial point of view, a more wide-ranging benevolence may well be counter-productive.

More useful has been the moral message, dinned into many generations of future workers, that one should beware the temptations of self and cleave fast to duty. Self-renunciation, whether for religious ends or in line with the post-religious demands of a secular pure morality, has been a prudent virtue for a work-directed culture to breed into a population with next-to-no time or energy for the pursuit of personal ends.

To come back to the ideal of the educated person in a post-productivist age. Is there any way of characterising his or her other-orientated qualities other than in traditional, 'moral' terms? Two of the items on the list I gave above fit ill into this way of thinking. Being friendly and having a sense of humour are not typically regarded as 'moral' qualities in the way that truthfulness is, or respect for property. There is no Commandment to get on well with people or to see the funny side of life. Yet although we have no obligations over these matters, there is no doubt that being approachable rather than forbidding and being humour-ful, not -less, are dispositions that help us all to get along together. True, the work-centred society may not have had much need of them over the centuries, but a broader stance to social life would value them more highly.

There are many other virtues that transcend traditional moral codes. We prize a more spontaneous warm-heartedness and beneficence and gratitude than their duty-motivated counterparts. We admire generosity – of spirit or in goods – when obligation does not enjoin it. We set a premium on erotic love and intimacy in personal relationships even though no Moral Law commands this.

Until the late 1970s most moral philosophers confined their investigations to moral obligations, their meaning, ontological status and justifiability. Since that time horizons have widened considerably. An ethics of moral rules has been supplemented by an ethics of the virtues. Of course, the earlier type of philosophising far from advocated obedience to a traditional moral code. Often following Kantian and/or utilitarian lines of argument, it explored the possibility of a rational set of moral principles enabling one to sift out traditional elements which prove rationally unjustifiable – to do with the alleged iniquity of masturbation, for example, or premarital sex. But despite its enlightened attitude towards autonomous thinking about moral matters, this type of moral philosophy was extraordinarily confined in the range of phenomena with which it dealt: such things as truthtelling, promise-keeping, justice, benevolence, respect for liberty, non-maleficence. From the late 1970s onwards increasing numbers of moral philosophers – who now began to drop this title, preferring 'ethics' to 'moral philosophy' as the name of their field – turned their attention to virtues of character, like courage, self-control, temperance (as the regulation of one's bodily appetites for food, drink, sex), love and friendship, self-confidence, generosity. Aristotle began to vie with Kant as prime historical source of inspiration. Nietzsche shook off his somewhat Nazi associations and was promoted to the front bench of modern moral philosophers. Like him, contemporary thinkers have found the broader ethical territory they were seeking in the sunny landscape of Greek ethics.

It is probably not coincidental that this philosophical recoil from older ways of conceiving morality took place at the same time as productivism came under serious challenge. If work is central to life, life must be built around obligations, both those of work itself and those of the orderly domestic routines which a work-regime demands. As paid employment begins to lose its hegemony, other personal qualities than those associated with it find new favour. Aristotle mapped the virtues suitable for a community of leisured persons who could leave heteronomous work to servants. Outside Knightsbridge and Bishops Avenue, Hampstead, we are far from this today. But if we are indeed moving towards Scenario 2, the interpersonal qualities we will need in this less busy world will bring us that bit closer to Greek ideals, that bit further from the morality of duty.

Education for personal fulfilment

From Mother Teresa to Felicity Kendal. From moral education to education for personal fulfilment. As it happens, the widening of ethical horizons with which we have just been dealing has brought us much of the way already. Aristotelian virtues are, indeed, primarily elements, and essential elements, of personal well-being, of *eudaimonia*. Courage, self-control and temperance help us to regulate our emotions of fear and anger and our physical appetites. Without them we would not be able to lead a fulfilling life. But they do not serve only our own interests, certainly not our interests construed narrowly in some self-centred way. As a social being, living in a community of other social beings, my ability to manage my feelings and desires is beneficial also to those around me.

Morality, as recent centuries have understood it, separates itself off sharply from self-concern. On the one side: my moral obligations, what I morally ought to do. On the other: my own interests, the goals I am free to follow once my moral duties are met. There are complications, of course. Some have wanted to make the meeting of their moral responsibilities their highest personal goal. And, as we have seen, there have been individual differences in the relative weights placed on morality and self-interest in one's life: strenuous moralists have left little space for the self and its temptations; while some of those with a more minimalist conception of morality, whose content consists of largely negative duties of restraint from harm and interference, have been able to spend their lives largely on their own affairs as long as they have been respectful of others in these ways. These variations apart, a key feature of the ethical tradition we have inherited has been the clear division it has made between morality and the self.

Familiar though it is, this is not the only perspective we can adopt on the ethical life. In an alternative deriving from Greek, not least Aristotelian, thought, self-concern and concern for others are not sharply differentiated. We have found this in the operation of the virtues, my courage, self-control and temperance benefiting not only myself but also those around me. We find it, too, in the more intimate of our personal relationships – in friendship, family life, sexual love. Although in all these spheres it may be possible – at a pinch – to try to keep self-interest on one side of the moral ledger and moral duty on the other, the shared attachments and pursuits typical of these relationships make it more natural to talk of what 'we' think and do than to atomise the 'we' into 'I' plus 'you'. A third area in which this separation is hard to make is that of activities in which we cooperate with others for shared ends – team games, work in a school or hospital, scientific research. In fulfilling my own ends, I am also fulfilling yours. Again, no neat dissection is possible.

There is nothing educationally amiss in bringing children up to put their own concerns somewhere near the centre of their existence, provided that we work with a conception of self-love generous enough to merge with altruism in the ways just suggested. We only recoil from the notion, insofar as we do, because, I suspect, we are still operating from within the tradition that keeps 'morality' and 'self-interest' in tidy compartments. If self-interest is to be unalloyed with anything that smacks of concern for others, it may be treated as excluding participation in relationships and activities which merge the two motivations. What does this leave us with? One: physical pleasures, shorn of social frameworks – sensations of eating, drinking, sex, athletic activity, minus the socialising, collaboration or intimate affection which usually accompany them. Two: the enjoyments of personal prestige and recognition. In other words, we edge closer to the picture of personal fulfilment that has come down to us as the flipside of our moralistic culture: a mix, with varying elements according to taste, of *Playboy*, *The Sun* and *Hello!* magazine.

Parents and teachers need to bring children up with a richer vision of their own well-being than this, one in which social attachments appear at virtually every point.

A life of well-being is, as we saw in Chapters 1 and 3 (above, pp 5, 45), one in which the individual broadly meets his or her major goals in life. In modern liberal societies, as we also saw, these goals are not ineluctably ascribed by the mores of the community but determined by the individual. This accounts for the important place that personal autonomy should have among the aims of education in a liberal society. On this view, with the aim of their flourishing in mind, children are brought up to decide themselves what the major orientations of their life will be – which patterns of personal relationships, including sexual relationships; which activities; which, if any, religious commitments, etc. If we reject the over-simple dichotomy between morality and self-interest, education for autonomy cannot be associated with the latter rather than the former. Not all of a child's future life will be the province of personal choice. No parent or teacher will lead children to think that whether they lie or keep their promises is wholly up to them. Children will learn due sensitivity to others' claims and interests. In part, this will come about from their preparation for autonomy, given that the activities and personal attachments they come to endorse will for the most part help others to flourish as well as themselves.

Education for autonomy

The broad educational aim should now be reasonably clear. What, more specifically, does it involve? What do parents and teachers and cultural educators need to bear in mind?

I would stress six things:

[1] If people are self-determiners, there is likely to be massive variation across the population in preferred ways of life and constituent activities and commitments. Children must be brought up to expect this and to welcome it. Diversity is something to be celebrated, not regretted – always given the baseline assumption I have been making throughout of due regard for others' well-being.

[2] Despite the diversity, everyone has certain basic needs which must be met if they are each to flourish. These have to do with such things as health, education, income, housing, security, liberty, social involvement and recognition. Children will have to be brought to realise the crucial importance of these things in their own and others' lives. And not only to realise this in an intellectual sense, but also, not least in their own case, to learn how to take steps to ensure that these needs are met.

[3] Since autonomy demands choices among alternatives, educators will have to introduce children to broad ranges of possibilities from which to select. Children will have to be given sufficient understanding of options to put them in a good position to be self-determining. Remember, too, that the options cover all kinds of activity, relationships, wider attitudes, e.g. towards religion. This brings with it extensive intellectual demands on the learner.

[4] These demands increase once we reflect that children need to know something about the social horizons within which they make their autonomous choices. These choices are not made in the abstract, according to some ideal template: they have to be realistic options in the actual circumstances of the learner's life. This requires some understanding of these social circumstances, of the culture and its institutions. This is a point reinforced once we dwell on the socially-sensitive nature of the autonomy aim: if promoting others' well-being is intertwined with one's own, one needs this understanding of society for their sake, too.

[5] Understanding options and social horizons is not sufficient equipment for the autonomous life. Children's practical rationality also has to be developed. They need to know how to go about achieving the goals they set themselves, how to identify obstacles and overcome them, how much to compromise when their ideal goals cannot be met, how, more generally, to deal with the conflicts of value endemic in the autonomous way of life. All this points to a practical dimension in home and school education. Of course, this practical rationality brings further demands on factual or theoretical knowledge in its train, in the shape of knowledge of means and obstacles. But it is not reducible to factual knowledge. A vital and sometimes neglected part of children's upbringing is helping them – once all the relevant factual knowledge is in the net – to make their own judgments about what to do.

The place in this of weighing conflicting values cannot be overemphasised. It is present in one's life both more globally and more particularly. Life is short; one cannot do everything; one has to strike one's own personal balances between the importance one attaches to friendship, to family life, to the arts, to civic involvement, etc. In specific situations one may have to weigh engaging in a project of one's own against meeting a friend's need. One may have to choose between two job-offers with contrasting pros and cons. Somehow – how? –

children need to be inducted into the complexities of all these sorts of conflict-resolution.

[6] Practical rationality is, as Aristotle has taught us, the pivotal virtue of a flourishing life. But there are also more specific personal qualities which it demands – and which educators need to cultivate in their charges. The autonomous life is built around self-chosen activities and relationships. To succeed in these, one needs a measure of commitment to the ends embedded in them; confidence that one can overcome the obstacles in their way; the strength of purpose to resist temptations; the moral courage to cleave to one's commitments in the face of opposing social pressure. In addition, one needs intellectual virtues like clarity of thought, objectivity, independence of mind to help orientate oneself in the more ratiocinative aspects of personal fulfilment.

The place of work among educational aims

I have dealt with the two ways in which we might take the notion of educating children to lead the good life – one to do with concern for others, the other with personal well-being. As we have seen, although our cultural tradition has tended to prise these apart into the mutually excluding spheres of morality and self-interest, there is a more attractive alternative which keeps them inextricable.

Scenario 2 brings with it a gradually decreasing role for heteronomous paid employment in people's lives. Educational aims should reflect this. We are not talking about a Utopia, or, for some, a Dystopia, in which heteronomous work is no more, but a society in which the centrality assumption is increasingly under challenge, and in which self-directed activities and relationships fill more and more of one's life.

There is a strong case, as we have seen, for replacing the morality/self-interest dualism with an ethic which brings personal flourishing more centre-stage. A culture dominated by the centrality of work cannot do this. It has been built round a morality of obligation, with personal concerns – in the popular conception of which physical pleasures have loomed large – relegated to the margins. As the centrality assumption comes under challenge, an education system appropriate to it should shift in the direction of personal aims. Increasingly, work-related aims should find their place within a larger framework of well-being aims.

Let me pick up from point [3] in the list above. If children are to become autonomous adults, their education must open up horizons on all sorts of possible major goals which they may wish to pursue. These will include activities and relationships. Work goals are a sub-set of activity goals. Not all activities, as we saw earlier in the book, involve work. Enjoying a novel or a film need not, and neither does socialising or walking on the downs. Children will be introduced to activities of these types, as well as to work options.

Among the latter, we need to make the by now familiar distinction between autonomous work, engagement in which constitutes a major goal in one's life, and heteronomous work, which lacks this feature. Children need to be introduced to a wide range of possibilities in the sphere of autonomous work – from work, usually paid work, which directly benefits others, as a farmer, a teacher, a nurse, a shopkeeper, to creative and intellectual activities in the arts and sciences. The options will also embrace types of heteronomous work – e.g. kinds of paid employment or housework – which may still play a part in a flourishing life, given that their disadvantages are sufficiently outweighed by other considerations.

In addition to kinds of work in this more substantive sense, there are also higher-order options to which pupils should be introduced. I mean by this that they should explicitly be brought to understand significant logical distinctions in the area – between activities in general and work activities in particular; between work and paid work; between autonomous and heteronomous work; between general types of paid work like core versus peripheral employment; between paid work and voluntary work. Until now, young people have been urged towards a single pattern of work, that is, full-time paid employment of as high status as possible in their circumstances. They need to be less confined. A higher-order enlargement of options will help in this.

The point of opening up these various options is partly informative – to make pupils aware of possibilities; and partly reflective – to encourage them to think of benefits and disbenefits, so that they are adequately equipped to give their preferences appropriate status within their system of goals. It should go without saying that the range of work, autonomous and constrained, to which children are to be introduced should be unrestricted. Given a principle of equal respect for all children, the traditional view in some educational systems that working class children need to be exposed only to working-class job possibilities, will be out of court. Making children aware of work-related options is a task that the school can and should share with the family. Broadly speaking, the more sophisticated part of this can be left to schools. These are in a better position to introduce pupils to forms of work dependent on mastery of some subject-matter, e.g. kinds of paid employment requiring a background in science, or the creative work of artists and scholars.

As well as an understanding of different forms of work – those selectable as options – pupils will also need, as we saw in item [4] in our list, an understanding of the social background in which choices are to be made. This includes the operations of the economy in its various articulations, as well as the technological-scientific basis on which it rests. This is essential background knowledge both for pupils' own self-directed choices and for their developing interests in helping to satisfy the needs and preferences of other people.

Another educational objective is acquainting pupils with views about the place of work especially in their own culture, but also in other cultures, and in human life more generally. For British children this will mean becoming aware of the traditional work ethic and the centrality assumption which has emanated from it. Aims to do with understanding are inextricable at this point from those to do with reflection on values: children need not merely to know what people think about the place of work, but also to come to their own conclusions about this. This will be part of encouraging a wider reflectiveness about their own and others' well-being, becoming broader and deeper as they grow older.

In Chapter 2 we also briefly discussed ecological implications for the doctrine of work, especially the dwindling world resources available to keep consumption as high as it has been and the pollution which this high consumption has brought in its train. Pupils need both to be inducted into relevant knowledge and understanding in this area and to reflect on the place of environmentally-costly pursuits in human well-being generally and in their own hierarchy of goals in particular.

Careers and life-plans

For many young people the traditional work culture has brought in its train the centrality not only of work in general, but also of a *career*. Children have often been brought up to view their life as a whole, stretching out before them, with retirement and death in the far distance, but the bulk of it centred around a series of jobs offering progressively more scope, interest and income. They have been encouraged to see their lives as the gradual working out of a personal career plan.

That a flourishing human existence should be built around a life-plan has been built into certain philosophical accounts of personal well-being, notably that of John Rawls in *A Theory of Justice* (Rawls, 1971, ch VII). In White 1982 (pp 56–57), I worked with a similar notion in sketching out aims for education. I have since come to realise that the link between life-planning and well-being is probably contingent rather than necessary (White, 1990, pp 85–89). A flourishing life is, among other things, one in which one's major goals are broadly met. *A fortiori*, this is also true of a flourishing life based on personal autonomy. But there is nothing here about how the goals have been arrived at – by incorporation in a long-term plan, or more spontaneously. People differ on this dimension. With luck, towards either end of the continuum they can lead a fulfilling life. There is no need to privilege the planners in this regard when those who take life more as it comes could, given good fortune, fare just as well.

In a work-dominated culture one can understand how the life-plan conception has come to be taken for granted. Not that, historically, it has always been associated with the notion of autonomous well-being. Two or three centuries ago, life-planning was necessary to meet one's religious/moral obligations towards God: one had to render account of how usefully one had laboured in his service. Allowing oneself to be blown hither and thither by more spontaneous impulses was hardly consonant with seriousness of purpose.

The secular work culture which a more religious age has bequeathed us still assumes that life is best built around a life-plan in the shape of a career, although its ethical framework often now has more to do with personal happiness than moral demands.

A more liberal view of the good life allows more room for the short-term and spontaneous. Recent shifts in philosophical and in socio-economic conceptions have both moved in the same direction. While philosophers (e.g. Williams, 1981, p 35) have broken the link between life-planning and individual well-being, changes in the labour market have helped to erode prospects of 'a job for life'. Of course, a more uncertain pattern of employment is not necessarily a bonus, often quite the contrary. But the cultural change that we are witnessing here can be shaped in a benign direction. If material insecurities brought about by the demise of jobs for life can be removed by social policy initiatives, the less tram-lined vision of personal futures can lead to new types of fulfilment. People will, if they wish, find it easier to live less instrumentally, with an eye on where they hope to be in ten, twenty or thirty years time. They can have more time for present or soon-to-be-present enjoyments.

As Giddens (1995, ch 5) has pointed out, the welfare state, as we have come to know it in Britain in the twentieth century, is in effect an adjunct of productivism. If work is to be central to our existence, social policy must be built around this. The normal expectation of forty plus years of full-time employment is preceded by a period of state-funded schooling, a large part of whose purpose is preparation for work; it is accompanied by state benefits for those unfortunate enough not to find a job; and it is succeeded by a period of state-supported retirement. This already imposes a skeletal life-plan on virtually the whole population. With the work culture now in probable abatement, these rigidities can be expected to soften. As Giddens advocates, there is a strong case for bluntening the sharp edge between paid work and retirement at age 60 or 65. And as we shall see, when we look more specifically at the future role of the school, there are good reasons for bringing into prominence forms of learning more associated with present enjoyments than equipment for a career.

Gender issues

One last point – again, triggered by Giddens (1995, ch 7). The age of the work ethic has been deeply gendered, men living out their fate at work, women in the home. In a post-productivist society, things are bound to change. Feminist pressure for women to take paid employment, and on equal terms with men, may have seemed to tilt things even further towards a work-dominated society. Perhaps in the short term it has indeed done so. But, like Thatcherism in the 1980s, which had this aim quite explicitly, it is likely, if Scenario 2 comes on stream, to yield in time before the cultural shift against the work ethic.

Unlike Thatcherism, feminist pressure on paid employment has been accompanied by other strands in feminist thinking which challenge conventional attitudes to work. I am thinking here of the celebration of traditional feminine virtues to do with concern and caring for those around one, with maintaining and fostering relationships, with cooperativeness and practical rationality in the conduct of everyday life. What is significant is that, as indicated above on p 77, these virtues have been advocated not only for women, but as part of a new model for living applicable to both sexes. Traditional masculine qualities associated with the career-mindedness and camaraderie of a working life – instrumental rationality and backing off from emotion, ambitiousness to get on, rivalry with other men and collective attachment to macho values – are now seen more clearly for what they are: cultural products, not the expressions of congenital maleness. Feminism joins forces with other underminers of the work ethic to make men and women more alike. For both sexes, Scenario 2 will increasingly see home and the family life, friendships and activities based in and around it as the hub of most individuals' existence. Just as schools are likely to give ground, as we saw earlier, to families as vehicles of education, so, more generally, the workplace will begin to yield to the home.

Educationally, this should bring with it a greater homogeneity in the character-formation of boys and girls. Aims of education are not always explicit. Although no school or education ministry in recent times has included in its public statement of aims the cultivation of different personal qualities for different sexes, the fact of cultural pressure for differentiation, filtered through family upbringing, is well-known. A shift away from productivism should help to temper this. Better still would be to make the gentler ethic for both sexes an *explicit* educational lodestone.

NOTES

1. Felicity Kendal is a British actress, well-known for her appearances in *The Good Life*, a television series about a young couple who had dropped out of the rat-race in favour of suburban self-sufficiency.

FIVE

Education and work: vehicles of learning

WORK AND LEARNING

So much for aims of education in Scenario 2 and the place of work-related aims among these. I want to turn in a moment to how these aims are to be realised, whether by families, schools or other social vehicles.

But before that, a few words on the conceptual relationship between learning and work.

Many types of learning involve work. John Dewey's Laboratory School in Chicago was built around occupations found in the wider society such as small-scale farming, cooking or woodwork (Dewey 1915). In learning the required skills, children at the same time not only learnt rudiments of literacy and numeracy, but also developed self-confidence and cooperativeness.

Dewey's school, as Skillen (1996, p 223) reminds us, 'was predicated on an assumption of human work as the central social activity' – the very assumption under challenge in this book. We will come back to it later when we look at schools in particular. For the present, the focus is on the broader concept of learning.

Learning can involve work even where the work is not tied to occupation, as in Dewey. Children can learn arithmetic in a more conventional way by working through exercises on long multiplication. This fits the broad definition of 'work' we have been using in this book, as activity engaged in with some end-product in mind: the children are doing the sums in order to reach the correct answers.

Much, perhaps most, of the learning favoured in schools is a form of work. Pupils draw maps, examine historical evidence, thresh about in the water in trying to swim, build apparatus, translate sentences into French. They do these things at least partly in order to get results, to produce something.

While it is undeniable that they are working, it is not always so obvious that they are learning. We need to distinguish activities associated with learning from learning proper. Learning is an achievement. One comes to know some-thing of which one was ignorant before – or in the case of learning to be con-fident or tolerant, one comes to acquire a disposition that one did not have, or have in such measure, before.

Some 'learning' activity does not lead to learning. Some children, asked to work through exercises on long multiplication, know how to do this already. They have grasped it intellectually and have already had adequate practice in consolidating the skill. They are working, but not learning. A lot of what goes on in classrooms seems to be like this. In some cases the main preoccupation of a poor teacher can be to keep his or her class hard at work, 'with their heads down'. Whether they advance in understanding or capability can become a sec-ondary consideration.

This said, I would not wish to deny for a moment that much of what chil-dren learn comes about, and perhaps could only come about, through produc-tive activity, through work.

But is work *necessary* for learning to take place? Can one learn something without engaging in an activity seen as instrumental to some end-product? Learning, remember, is an achievement, not itself an activity. It implies one has come up to a new mark in possessing something – knowledge, understanding, skill, an attitude or personal quality – one lacked before. Learning can come about in quite informal ways. A friend tells me the latest political news. As a result I learn from her that the US president has decided to stand for a new term. This is a bona fide example of learning: an hour ago I knew nothing of the president's decision; now I know it. At the same time, it has required no work on my part. I have undergone no productive activity on the way to acquir-ing the knowledge. The only activity I have engaged in is chatting to my friend. In the course of this, as a by-product, I heard from her the news about the president. The activity itself, the chatting, was something done for its own sake, something enjoyable in itself without any thought of how it might be used for some extrinsic purpose.

Breaking the often-assumed connexion between learning and work via counterexamples like this is an important move in recasting education to fit a post-productivist age. We should become clearer than we often are that it is learning, not working, that is central to education. Remember, too, that educa-tion is not to be identified with schooling. We are taking it as upbringing. Once we do so, it becomes more obvious how much it depends on non-work forms of learning. So much of what a very young child learns comes from what its parents tell it. The basic stages in learning one's mother tongue have a lot to do with hearing hosts of different words used properly in context. Effortlessly, children come to know what things are called; if they make mistakes, they are corrected and so come to get things right. All this is, for them, just as much a by-product of enjoyable interactions within the family as my learning that the president is standing for re-election is unintended spin-off from a conversa-tion.

Granted, parents may and do inject into early learning questions like 'Now, do you remember what other animals have long ears?' or 'If I take away these three cards, how many will you have left?' Some children will answer immediately. But the more a child has to think it through, the more work-like the occasion becomes. This is because the child is engaging in an activity (thinking), intending to bring about an end-product (the answer to the parent's question).

Zealously pedagogical parents aside, most early learning fortunately comes about more spontaneously, through ordinary social experience. And not only early learning. At whatever age, so much of what we come to know is by this route.

This is true not only for factual knowledge like the president's decision or the names of eating implements, but also for other things one learns. Understanding the reasons for things, for instance. The conversation a child hears at home is likely to bear from time to time on people's motives for doing what they do or on causal explanations of physical phenomena, like plants withering (through lack of rain) or the television not working (because it is not plugged in). At more sophisticated levels, we can come to understand something of why Britain's economy is sluggish or why global warming is occurring. True, the more complex and theoretical the understanding, the more effort (work) one may have to put into acquiring it. But the general point remains, that where what is attained is a deeper understanding of some subject-matter, work does not always come into the picture.

This is also true of skill-learning, at least in part. Children can pick up all sorts of things through seeing their parents cooking, decorating, gardening, cleaning the car, handling social situations. True, they will need more than this to acquire these skills themselves – plenty of practice in them, for a start. But what they pick up either just by looking on or, in addition, by being told what to do and why, is all helpful to this end.

Finally, the acquisition of attitudes, emotional responses, traits of character. So much of this has to do with learning by example – good or bad. There is no need to labour this point as it is very familiar: insensibly, we imbibe our racism, our vanity, our cheerfulness, our sense of humour from those around us – family not least, friends, the media. Work does not come into it.

Most of the non-work-based learning just described is not the product of teaching. It requires people from whom to learn, but these need have no pedagogical intent. They can certainly tell you all sorts of things, but telling is not always teaching. Sometimes, too, even telling is absent: the learner learns simply by using his or her senses.

Where teaching *does* come into the story, how far does the learning it produces come about through work? *Teachers* are workers, of course – not only school teachers, but anyone who sets about teaching someone something, however informally. This flows from our understanding of the concept of teaching. 'Teaching' is what philosophers have called a 'task-achievement' term. It has these two aspects. A school teacher can be teaching a class all afternoon (task), but at the end of the day come to the conclusion that she has taught them nothing (achievement). In the task sense of the term, to teach is to engage in certain activities with the intention of bringing about learning in someone. In the achievement sense, it is to have been successful in this intention. Although teaching in the task sense can sometimes fail, as we have seen, the two senses nevertheless involve each other, in that the task must aim at the achievement and the achievement could not come about without the task. Teaching differs from learning in that, although both terms connote some sort of achievement, that is, bringing about learning on the one hand and acquiring knowledge, etc. on the other, only teaching is necessarily an activity: as we saw above, learning can come about in other ways. Teaching is, moreover, necessarily a form of work, since the activity in which teachers engage is designed to bring about a certain end-product, i.e. learning.

Teachers work. But when they are being (successfully) taught by a teacher, need learners? Not always. Teachers must intend that their pupils learn, but they need not intend that they engage in work on the way to this. For one thing, they can simply tell them things in an attractive way. Their students can effortlessly get drawn into accounts of historical events, authors' lives and scientific inventions. Teachers can also consciously act as ethical models, knowing that by showing children respect and giving them encouragement and recognition, their own attitudes and behaviour may be insensibly transmitted.

Play has long been a staple in the child-centred teacher's repertoire. It has been heavily criticised as a teaching method over the years, on the – correct – grounds that it does not automatically lead to learning. On the other hand, it may sometimes do so. Parents and teachers of younger children know all about the potential of games and game-like activities to establish concepts, extend vocabulary, develop number skills, and much else besides. This, again, is a form of non-work learning. Unlike some other forms of this like being told things, it involves overt activity on the child's part, but from the child's point of view this is activity engaged in for its intrinsic delightfulness and not because of any end-product it may bring about.

Closely akin to playing is enjoying works of art. Parents and teachers encourage children to read stories, poems, dramas and novels. Parents more often than teachers also let them see films for educational (as well as other) reasons. A wealth of learning can be acquired in this way – factual information, a better understanding of human nature, emotional refinement, ethical sensitivity and aesthetic awareness. While something of the same could be said about painting and music, the many-sided learning which worthwhile literature and films facilitate is well-attested. As with play, children are attracted into artistic activities of this sort for intrinsic reasons. They learn all sorts of things on the way, but setting themselves to do this is never in their thoughts.

These are some of the non-work forms of learning that parents and teachers can encourage. What I find remarkable about them all is that once school begins they are progressively demoted, discouraged, in some quarters even denigrated, as compared with types of work-based learning. Children quickly learn that they are at school in order to work. School is not meant to be fun – playing games, conversing, listening to riveting material from the teacher, spending hours absorbed in a novel, watching films. In a work-dominated culture its purpose is more serious.

If we are indeed moving into Scenario 2, however, should we not put learning first and heteronomous work second? Work-based learning will still have its place, indeed a large place – the closer to autonomous rather than heteronomous work, the better. I shall come back to this in looking at the role of the school in particular. But where non-work types of learning produce rich results, it would be silly not to make more use of them than we currently do. The rich results are not all to do with specific items learnt: tilting the scales somewhat away from work-based learning will itself help to wean children from a belief that work is and must be central to their existence.

A closer look, now, at the main agencies of education and the part they can each play in preparing children for Scenario 2. I begin with parents.

PARENTS' RESPONSIBILITIES

Parents are a child's first, and chief, educators. The guidelines given above on educational aims apply in the first instance to them. It is they who start the child on the way to a fulfilling life as an autonomous person responsive to others' needs and interests. It is they who begin to equip him or her with the linguistic competences, understanding of the social and natural world, and qualities of character necessary to attain this. It is they who first shape the child's perceptions of the world of work and attitudes toward it.

It stands to reason that what parents do in educating their children should be coordinated with what schools do. In Britain, as in other countries, this coordination has traditionally been deficient – and for several reasons. Family life has been seen as a private matter, beyond the legitimate interference of the state. Children have been protected against gross neglect, abuse, or danger to health, but beyond these minima, parents have been broadly free to bring up children as they will. Until the pressure for a National Curriculum culminated in the Education Reform Act of 1988, teachers and schools, too, were left with extensive powers, at least in theory, to teach pupils what they saw fit. Increasing homogeneity across schools in recent years – first at LEA level, then at national – has made possible policies on parent-school collaboration. Parents have been involved, for instance, in teaching basic skills and in home-school contracts.

To date schools have been dominant partners. Parental help has been welcomed insofar as it has promoted the work of the school. But since schools themselves have been so much under the thumb of the work culture, parental involvement has been in effect subordinated to it, too.

This is also true of the coincidence between parental ambitions for their children and school aims. Many parents have wanted schools to equip their children for 'a good job', variously interpreted according to class and cultural expectations. Secondary schools, especially, have responded by making success in public examinations central to their work.

In Scenario 2 home-school relationships need to be reconceptualised on more equal terms. In place of the hierarchy: work society > schools > families, pride of place should go to the overall aims of education, with parents and teachers as co-agents of their attainment. If anything, given the greater educative influence that parents have, the balance should be tilted their way; but this is less important than that both parties work together to bring children up as members of a society no longer dominated by heteronomous work.

Crudely, what has happened to date is that a child's pre-school life within the family has been broadly excluded from the work culture. It has been a time for play, for intimacy, for freedom and indulgence – before the thickening of Wordsworth's prison-house shades. Primary school transmutes play into work, its heteronomy and hegemony typically increasing as the child grows older. The role of the family then becomes split: partly a haven of non-work, pre-school values; and partly an adjutant of the school in its socialisation into the work culture.

Although there is a gamut of cases here, at the extreme these pre-school, family values are polar opposites of work values. Where the latter pivot around constraint, the former celebrate liberty. All too soon, one's children are going to be subjected to 'the grind', 'the treadmill', 'the rat race'. Let them enjoy themselves while they can! Early childhood is a time for playing, not working; for doing what one wants (within reasonable limits), not doing what others want, even for being spoilt a little. Later, the more the pressures of schoolwork grow, with homework and exam-preparation added to the usual daily toll, the more incumbent it is on parents to preserve this precious psychological space.

This is, as I say, at the extreme. Not every family makes the contrast with the work-world so stark. Whatever the sociological complexities of our present ways of life, in Scenario 2 the traditional values of home and school will come closer together. The play-work duality will give way to a common encouragement of desirable *activity*. Following our by now familiar logical subdivision, this will include non-work activity; autonomous work; and heteronomous work. Both schools and families will deal in each category. We will come to schools later. As for families, it would help if parents defined their role more clearly than they often do at present and consciously encouraged these various forms of activity, duly balanced in importance, bearing in mind the continuities between their own work and that of teachers.

Their pre-school and young school-age children can be caught up in a range of non-work activities, from verbal interactions through physical and mental games to listening to stories or looking at picture books. Autonomous work cannot be possible with children as young as this in the full sense of 'autonomy', since they are as yet incapable of choosing major life-goals in the light of a broad understanding of alternatives. But gradually, as their understanding of means-ends relationships grows, children can take part in self-chosen activities with a clear end product in view – a birthday card, a sweet-dispensing 'machine', a road system. This is the seed of autonomous work, if still far from its full flowering. The first introduction into heteronomous work can be made, as well, although the task will be different. I am tempted to say that non-work activities and proto-autonomous work can be encouraged without limit, while the parent's task vis-à-vis heteronomous work is more delicate. In Scenario 2 children are no longer to be brought up to accept its centrality as a fact of life. Yet heteronomous work will still probably be an ineluctable, if not now domi-nant, part of their lives – although as far as possible its activities will be recon-ceptualised so as to cohere with autonomy's demands (see p 54 above). Children should be prepared for this, too – by parents' welcoming their first, imagination-impregnated, attempts to help one wash the car, for instance, and, later, by insisting that they tidy their room, clean the bath after them and help with household chores.

Families do all these kinds of things already, of course; but as we edge, if we do edge, towards Scenario 2, it would be good if parents could link them more consciously to the demands of the post-productive society.

Activity, then, becomes the central thread of both pre-school and school days, replacing the worn-out duo, work and play. There should be no difficul-ty from a psychological point of view in engaging children in (worthwhile) activity, given their natural propensities to be active. Some parents might find this harder, perhaps through a deficient understanding of how children tick, not realising their own crucial role in structuring patterns of activity for them. They may leave them too much to 'amuse themselves', not seeing how this con-signs them to boredom or the unhelpful fantasies of excessive televiewing. In the work culture we have known, parents, too, are often too little with their children, or, when they are, too jaded to do much for them. If Scenario 2 comes about, parents will work less. This will both give them more time and energy for their proper educative functions *and* enable them to be different role-models for their children. For many children brought up in a productivist culture, working parents doing unattractive jobs, about which they complain endlessly and from which they wish themselves into greener pastures, must sometimes be *anti*-role-models. In post-productivist society, as adults come to have more time for their own activities, children will be acquainted and re-acquainted day in, day out, with more engaging visions of how to live.

Educatively, parents have a many-sided task in this area. Two of those sides we have already looked at: channelling children's energies into work and non-work activities; and acting as role-models for how work-activities can be balanced out against others. A third has to do with character-formation, with taking early steps in equipping children with the personal qualities needed to flourish in Scenario 2.

Of course, some personal qualities come with the first two – enthusiasm and commitment to enjoyable activities, self-confidence and cooperativeness acquired through performing them, admiration of adults and the desire to follow in their footsteps. But also important is the proper regulation of one's bodily appetites and emotions, that is, the acquisition of such virtues as temperance (in the Greek, not the Salvation Army sense, of control of one's innate desires for food, drink and sex), courage (which helps one to cope with one's fears), and self-control (which does the same for anger).

Temperance is an especially interesting virtue in the passage from productivism to post-productivism. If the flip-side of the industriousness exacted from children at school is often parental indulgence, a change in school culture away from excessive work should be matched by changes at home. Too much television; too many toys, computer games and other consumer goods on demand; too much fast food: many parents' misplaced kindness – or shelling out for a peaceful life – are well-known. Children need ethical stiffening against the temptations around them. In the more relaxed world of Scenario 2, their parents should be better able to attend to this. As well as shaping character, their work can also have an intellectual dimension, in making children more conscious of consumerism and its hidden persuaders. In this way parental education may play some part in reversing the overproduction of goods which has demanded so much, and such unnecessary, heteronomous work.

SCHOOLS AND WORK

Scenario 2 will bring with it greater continuity between home and school education, greater similarities between parents and teachers. Of course, teachers will expand the structures which parents lay down into intellectual edifices which parents lack the time or specialised understanding to create. But at root they will be, like parents, upbringers, shapers of the whole child, not crimped subject specialists.

They will share with parents their many-sided task of socialisation into post-productivist culture. Inducting into desirable activities will be the hub of both sets of endeavours. For both, heteronomous work-activities will be given their due weight, perhaps more than tradition has accorded them for the parent, but less – far less – for the teacher. I shall say more about this later.

Teachers can also be a new kind of model for the pupil. A 1996 survey showed British teachers working longer than the 48-hour week of the European Union's social chapter, with an average of over 50 hours for classroom teachers and between 55 and 61 hours for headteachers. Between 1994 and 1996 two hours a week was added to primary teachers' workload and 1.4 hours to secondary teachers'[1]. The drudge conception of the teacher familiar to us in Britain since Dickens' time has hardly yielded a picture of a fulfilled human life. If working hours decrease, teachers' included, the latter should not only be less pressed and jaded when working with children, but also have time to develop other interests. Like parents, they will project the message that life need not be all work, but could embrace a variegated and fulfilling pattern of more self-directed and more constrained activities, with a marked preponderance of the former.

Although much of the foreground emphasis will be on academic pursuits, character-education will be at the heart of the teacher's work, as it is of the parent's. The same personal qualities will be reinforced; the same virtues developed, filled out now in a more reflective direction as the pupil's intellectual horizons expand. The temperance whose first shoots the parent tended will be accompanied now by a deeper understanding of the economy and its consumerist blandishments. More generally, pupils will come to unify and prioritise the various dispositions into which, semi-atomically, they have been inducted, under the overarching aegis of practical rationality. The first responsibility of the teacher will be to guide them towards that destination. (White, 1990, ch 5).

In end-of-century Britain, this new vision of the school and of the teacher is not with us yet, to put it a touch mildly. In 1995, the former Department for Education was merged with the Department of Employment to form the new Department for Education and Employment (DfEE). In September of that year, the DfEE described its overall aim as being:

> To support economic growth and improve the nation's competitiveness and quality of life by raising standards of educational achievement and skill and by promoting an efficient and flexible labour market. (DfEE 1995a)

In a November 1995 document (DfEE 1995b, p1), this was declared to be 'the Government's principal aim for the education service at all levels and in all forms of learning'.[2]

Subordination of schools and colleges to the demands of the work culture could hardly be plainer. For the previous thirty and more years we had got used to a tension among educational aims, between the academic, the personal and the economic. For the moment the latter seems to rule supreme.

Whether or not this proves one of productivism's last throes before an about-turn towards Scenario 2 is at yet unknown. Meanwhile, let us fill out what schools could look like in that scenario.

The school's main vehicle for realising its educational aims is the curriculum. In Britain, since 1988 we have had a National Curriculum. Assuming it continues in some form, how might it be remodelled to fit the needs of post-productivism?

Remodelled it certainly should be. For all the intricate complexities of its original version – before Ron Dearing was brought in to hack clearings through it with his Civil-Service-issue machete, the basic framework is absurdly simple. Ten traditional school subjects, of which three – maths, science, and English – are 'core'. I remember, in Spring 1989, formally presenting to the University of Illinois at Urbana-Champaign the 'actual' brown envelope on the back of which Kenneth Baker, as Secretary of State for Education, had scribbled down the National Curriculum. I did not realise then, what we all know now, that the inspiration for this historic event came originally from Mrs

Thatcher's hairdresser, worried about his daughter's poor progress at a South London primary school. True, this fired Mrs Thatcher to put her money on something even more rudimentary than the National Curriculum we actually got: the three-subject core. It was only Kenneth Baker's wife, a former secondary teacher, who saved us from this. 'When I used to come back bloody and bowed from these meetings,' writes her husband of his interactions with the prime minister, 'she would say, "No, you must stick out for a broad-based curriculum." I think this is the first time I've mentioned that. I should have acknowledged her role in this much more'. (*The Daily Telegraph*, 1 June 1996).

Thanks to the courage, persistence and sheer intellectual acumen of Mr and Mrs Baker, we now have a National Curriculum of.... ten traditional school subjects. Among all these negotiations and blue-rinsings, no one seems to have given any consideration to what the curriculum should be about, to what its underlying aims should be. Except, perhaps, on second thoughts, Mrs Thatcher and her hairdresser. The three core subjects are all especially relevant to economic growth – at least, they are said to be. Although there is no interest in anything beyond the work society's requirements, at least there are clarity and unity of purpose in this suggestion. But what holds together its ten-subject competitor? What purpose is *this* meant to subserve?

It does, let us be fair, come with aims attached. All two lines of them. The first line says that the National Curriculum should promote 'the spiritual, moral, cultural, mental and physical development of students at school and of society'; the second adds that it should prepare them 'for the opportunities, responsibilities and experiences of adult life'. Is it possible to imagine a conciser, more accurate, more practically applicable account of the purposes of a nation's curriculum than this?

These two lines, so patently tacked on as an afterthought, are what now guide English and Welsh schools. They are what OFSTED's new school inspectors have foremost in mind in seeing whether a school is up to the job. Yet what the cloudy terms they embrace may be taken to mean is anyone's guess. The religious education lobby has been thrilled by the inclusion of 'spiritual'. It has been bending over backwards ever since to assure everyone that 'spiritual' is not necessarily connected with 'religious' and that believers and unbelievers alike are interested in life's great questions, where we are all going, what it all means, etc.

With its ten foundation subjects and its ten levels of attainment, the 1988 National Curriculum is a masterpiece of decimalised illogic. It has no aims to speak of. What pass as such – the two lines – have no perceptible relationship with the ten subjects for which they are supposed to give a rationale.

Scenario 2 will be better off without it. Not that bits of it, perhaps quite large bits, can't remain. Of course we will want children to learn some science, some history and so on. But *what* science and *what* history cannot sensibly be determined before asking what we might want them for. Aims must come first. Otherwise we get stuck, for instance, with the nonsense of the history curriculum with which we are now encumbered, whereby students can leave school exposed to no twentieth century history beyond a module on the causes of the Second World War. (A recent survey has shown that nearly one-third of British children aged ten to sixteen think Germany is the poorest country in Europe (*The Independent*, 10 June 1996)).

The basic defect of the National Curriculum is that its starting point was a list of subject areas, not reflection on where this vehicle was supposed to go. Foundation subjects are, after all, only means to ends. Whether they are the best means depends, again, on what the end is. Aims are inescapable. A replacement National Curriculum for Scenario 2 will put them first in every sense.

Before we turn to this, a final thought about the National Curriculum we have now and its relation to the work culture. Even before the merging of the two ministries into the DfEE bound the whole education service so firmly to economic exigencies, the National Curriculum had already tightened the strings. I am thinking not only of the attention it gave to the core subjects, but also of the way it reinforced the school's traditional ethos of heteronomous work. As remarked in Chapter 1, schools have not at all existed in an autonomous zone outside the work society. Traditionally, as soon as children have come to school at five – and increasingly earlier – they have been subjected to a work-regime totally beyond their control or preferences. Although in the earliest school years, non-work forms of learning – through play, listening to stories etc – have often been in evidence, children have soon found most of their school day taken up with school*work*. As they have moved from primary to secondary school, the work, still largely heteronomous, has grown more extensive, supplemented now with home-work and preparation for public examinations.

Through its complex system of targets to be met the National Curriculum has intensified this regime of work. Not least in the primary schools, now deliberately made more like secondary schools in being yoked to a strict subject framework. If it is headbreakingly unproductive to try to discern sensible *educational* aims behind the National Curriculum, as a vehicle of initiation into the work culture it makes far more sense.

How might it be remodelled to suit Scenario 2? I will not give a full account of this here, only pick out some key points. A more detailed account of a new national curriculum can be found in O'Hear and White (1991). This does not have work-related issues particularly in mind, but its general approach and most of its conclusions fit our present concerns.

Here are the key points:

[1] The starting point should be its underlying aims. I have outlined these above. We are educating children as citizens of a liberal democratic society and must think what kinds of personal qualities they need as such. These include more other-directed virtues, like truthfulness, cooperativeness, benevolence, non-maleficence etc, as well as ones more closely linked with personal fulfilment, like autonomy, confidence, commitment to one's projects, and practical

wisdom in the conduct of one's life. I indicated above the inadvisability of distinguishing too sharply between moral and personal/prudential values.

Aims to do with personal qualities generate aims to do with the acquisition of *knowledge and understanding*. To be benevolent, one has to know something about the particular situation, needs and preferences of those to whom one is being benevolent. If we are talking about small-scale acts of goodness towards family, friends, neighbours we will not have to draw on the understanding of geography, history, economics, current affairs or sociology necessary for benevolent concern on a global scale, towards the poor in the third world, for instance. This is only one example, based on one personal quality, but I hope the signpost it sets up in the direction of a school curriculum is visible enough. If we took other qualities, we would get more signposts. Personal autonomy, for instance. If people are to be part-authors of their lives, they need an understanding not only of the various major options before them, among which they are going to choose their own way forward – artistic pursuits, for instance, sports, business activities, public service, religious and sexual options; but also of the society, with all its opportunities and constraints, in which they are likely to be making these choices. Work-related understanding required by the autonomy aim is of: [a] differences between work activities and non-work activities and between autonomous and heteronomous work (this is a necessary ingredient in the student's understanding of options); [b] the broad range of types of paid employment available in the society; [c] the domestic and international economic systems; [d] the place of work in the culture and in human life.

As well as knowledge and understanding, personal qualities also require *skills*, types of know-how. Children won't get far, for instance, on the road to tolerance, cooperativeness or practical wisdom unless they know how to read, write and count. Logical skills like knowing how to construct, follow and criticise arguments are also important. Here, as elsewhere in this brief sketch, I give only one or two examples out of many.

[2] Note that I've said nothing yet about school subjects or any other feature of a traditional timetabled curriculum. That is because a timetabled curriculum is only a means to an end, a vehicle for further purposes. Where the 1988 National Curriculum began with the vehicle, the present account starts with the destination. Only now are we in a position to turn to procedures.

[2.1] In doing so, we should not assume that the timetabled curriculum is the only means of realising educational aims. It is well-known these days that *whole school processes* are another. The question for us is, then: how can the way a school is organised, its rules, its ethos help to promote the personal qualities, forms of understanding and skills mentioned in [1]?

Again, there is a fuller account of this in O'Hear and White (1991).

If preparation for membership of a liberal democratic society is the keystone aim, expectations about staff-staff, student-student, staff-student and staff-parent interactions can be shaped accordingly. Not all learning is work-based learning, as we saw above. Children can learn by example, through their day-to-day experience, how to treat others decently, how to hold courageously but not obstinately to their own point of view, how to collaborate appropriately with others in shared endeavours. Among other things, they will pick up all sorts of attitudes towards and perspectives on work.

As we saw earlier, in Scenario 2 teachers, like every other group, will be working fewer hours. If there is any professional group in present-day Britain which needs no reminding about the centrality of 'work', if it is not health care workers it is surely school teachers. The burdens which funding constraints on the one hand and the National Curriculum on the other have placed on them in recent years are well-known. English and Welsh teachers are unusual in the hours they are expected to work. In France, Germany and other countries their commitments are less. This makes more sense. If your job is to encourage others to learn, you need to be as fresh and stimulating as possible. A tradition like the English founded on a constant regression to the mean in drudgery needs to be replaced by something more functional. Present arrangements are bad for pupils in more than one way. Not only do they have overworked teachers, but – closer to our theme – they are presented day in day out with an ineluctable reminder of the centrality of work in the adult world.

If teachers' hours were reduced, this part of the hidden curriculum could project a quite different message. Young people come into teaching partly because they want to teach but also because they want to remain in the world of learning and the arts to which they have become attached in their sixth forms and universities. Many of them have ambitions as scholars, journalists, novelists, sportsmen and women, musical performers, actors, creative artists. They may try to play down the attractiveness of the long holidays when they apply for jobs, but the motive is there all the same. Imagine the release of all this creative energy if working patterns were changed! They could throw themselves with enthusiasm into their fewer hours work a day (which would themselves be more fulfilling if school had pupils' overall well-being more in their sights). Although they would still be constrained by the need to earn a living, what they did within this framework would match more closely the reasons why they chose teaching in the first place: it would flow from their autonomous choices. Their pupils would see at first hand what autonomous work could be like. After classes, teachers would have time to themselves to pursue their creative and other interests. This, too, could not fail to impress itself on children, helping to give them a picture of a society in which lives like this were the norm, as well as the personal resolution that when they make their way in the world they should settle for no less.

Students can pick up attitudes to work not only from their teachers – and, indeed, other workers around the school like caretakers and dinner ladies – but also from the place the school accords it in their own learning. It is largely up to the school (but also political bodies who decide on national curriculum frameworks) to decide whether, at one extreme, as much timetabled learning as possible should be (largely heteronomous)-work-based, or whether non-work-based learning is to be maximised. The former choice would be a powerful reinforcer of the centrality doctrine. The more deliberately a school encouraged appropriate forms of non-work learning, the less this doctrine would be taken for granted. Again, this is not the place for detailed specification. We have already looked at non-work learning via whole school processes. What about the timetabled curriculum? With very young children we may need to rethink the swing away from learning through play which is part of the current (and often justified) onslaught on 'progressive' or 'child-centred' education. Once children can read fluently, they can learn a very great deal, in a non-work way, from books. Under guidance, but left largely to themselves, they can move from story to story, especially, but not only, fictional, bearing in mind that biography and history can become just as enthralling. In Scenario 2 school libraries and public libraries would become key sites of learning.

The other way in which schools could deliberately change attitudes to work would be by tilting the balance from heteronomous classroom work more towards autonomous. For many children, schoolwork is something to be suffered rather than enjoyed. A first move away from this is to make the work enjoyable. It is still constrained, in that students have no option but to do it; but at least the time passes pleasantly. This parallels the work that many adults do, and will continue to do on Scenario 2. A second move away is when the work becomes so enjoyable that one would choose to do it even if it were not compulsory. This may not be full-blooded autonomous work, if we take this to be work with an end-product of major significance in one's personal hierarchy of preferences – like the work of autonomous artists or teachers. Few children are in a position to makes choices of this sort. But the second move I suggested is a step on the road to this; and as children grow older and take more responsibility for their own self-creation, something closer to the fuller-blown case can become possible, too.

[2.2] The timetabled curriculum is, of course, the major vehicle for realising educational aims. We should not assume that it must be arranged exclusively around school subjects, as there can be other timetablable vehicles. (So we still have not yet reached the favourite notion of the National Curriculum perm-specialists and other planners). Projects, topics, themes are all ways in which personal qualities and areas of understanding can be promoted. Personal and social education (PSE), that fast-growing area of the school curriculum throughout the eighties, for which the National Curriculum had next to no time, is an especially helpful means of delivering the aims appropriate to Scenario 2. There is perhaps no need to go into much more detail on the place that school subjects would have in this scheme. History, science, geography, mathematics, literature, social studies, technology, art, music and PE would all find a niche there, although there should be no automatic assumption as there is in the National Curriculum that all subjects (except modern languages in the case of the National Curriculum) should be taught to every child every year from the age of five. The content of each subject's curriculum would be chosen in accordance with the aims laid out above. For more details on all this, including comments on modern languages, creative arts activities, religious education, foreign literature in translation etc, see White (1990, chs 9,10).

There is probably no need, either, for me to spell out in detail here how the timetabled curriculum can promote aims specifically to do with work. PSE can engage students in thinking about the place of work in human life and the possible place of different kinds of work in their own lives. History and sociology can chart the origins and spread of the work culture. Science and technology can throw light on the kind of advanced industrial base on which our culture now rests. I will not say more about this here, since if the basic aims are accepted, it is not too difficult to work out how different subjects and other vehicles may contribute to their attainment.

REMAKING THE SCHOOL DAY

How much of the school day should the timetabled curriculum take up? In Britain, we do not often ask ourselves this question, taking it for granted that, with breaks, compulsory lessons last from early morning until mid- or late afternoon. In other countries there is often a shorter school day.

The long British one makes heteronomous work as central to most schoolchildren's lives as it is to adults'. Intended as such or not, it socialises them into the traditional work culture. Schools reflect in their own arrangements the centrality of work in the larger culture. Pupils are constrained, whether they like it or not, to come to school and to engage in various kinds of productive activity, homework as well as schoolwork, for most of their waking day. If the centrality assumption were challenged for schoolchildren, this would help to remove its hegemony in the culture overall – partly because the period of compulsory schooling is such a large slice of a human life, and partly because through its being challenged in the early years, dispositions can be built up which may lead to its erosion in the adult world.

Although I did not then see it that way, my first book *Towards a Compulsory Curriculum* (White 1973), written over twenty years ago, questioned the centrality assumption – not in general, but with regard to the school years. The main theme of the book is that in Britain we take for granted that children should be compelled to come to school and attend classes for six or seven hours a day between five and sixteen but we do not ask why compulsion of this extent is justified. *Prima facie*, it is not. For children as for adults the *ceteris paribus* assumption should be that they should be free to do what they want. On this view, any constraints on their liberty have to be justified in terms of some more important consideration. That there are legitimate overriders to children's liberty is not hard to show. Their own good is one such. Educators have to insist that children learn certain things, for if they did not learn them their own interests would be harmed. Reading and writing would be one example. But children are not to be brought up only on prudential lines, concerned with their own well-being. They are also to grow up morally good, sensitive also to others' interests. Considerations of possible harm to others in the absence of a moral education will impose a further justified constraint on their freedom to do what they want. In general, outside these justified restrictions on liberty, children should be left free to do whatever they want. This points in the direction of a shortening of the compulsory school day. The part which remained, perhaps a morning session, would be devoted to learning which is vitally important from the prudential and moral points of view. Children would then be free to take part in – but only if they chose to – a programme of voluntary activities in which they could pursue their own concerns. One source of this idea, but to be shorn of its ideological purposes, was the Young Pioneers organisation that I had seen in operation in the Soviet Union at the end of the 1950s. Soviet children had only a half day of compulsory schooling and could spend their free time in Pioneer circles learning to build radios or play the violin.

This gives the bare bones of the argument. Most of it is about the pupil's own good and its curricula implications rather than about moral goodness. I will come back to this later. There are various problems about this early account which I need not dwell on here: the somewhat starry-eyed picture of Soviet realities; the questionable prudence/morality dichotomy; the excessively thin conception of individual well-being. More relevant to present concerns is the inadequacy of the libertarian starting-point from which to question the extent of compulsion. I assumed that what went for adults in such matters also went for children: the principle of liberty, as I stated it – that people should *ceteris paribus* be allowed to do what they want without constraint – was applicable across the board. I did not press the argument back to ask why we should accept this principle. If I had done, I might have come to realise that it is difficult to see what could ground liberty as an intrinsically desirable good and that its value seems to reside in its being a necessary condition for the exercise of personal autonomy. But if this is so, while liberty is important for persons already autonomous, its value for people who are not yet autonomous or who never will be autonomous is still in question. And if, lastly, we can take it that the younger children are, the further back they are on the road towards becoming autonomous, the weaker becomes the libertarian basis for challenging compulsory schooling.

True, given both that autonomy is a matter of degree and that for pedagogical reasons children often need to be treated as more autonomous than they yet are, there is a case for leaving them with whatever liberty of action is appropriate as a condition of such autonomy, this sphere of freedom increasing as they grow older and capable of greater self-rule. But this does not yield the radical position of *Towards a Compulsory Curriculum* that there should be no compulsory schooling unless it can be shown to be a legitimate overrider of the child's liberty.

Even so, compulsory schooling *does* have to be justified, even if the starting-point is not libertarian. It seems to me now that there is a route – not necessarily the only one – and this is from a concern for the child's well-being. This concern came into the libertarian story too, of course, as I showed above, but the more adequate justification is more direct. If the child's well-being (in life generally) is to be promoted, certain basic needs have to be satisfied – for food, health, shelter, etc, as outlined in Chapter 3. Education is among these needs: if they are to flourish, children have to acquire all sorts of dispositions, skills and forms of understanding. In addition to the route from the child's own well-being, there are other possible routes originating from the well-being of other people. Various learnings on the child's part are necessary conditions of his or her growing up with altruistic inclinations.

This line of argument does not yet embrace compulsory schooling, only some kind of compulsory (i.e. unavoidable) education or upbringing. How this compulsory education is to be apportioned to different agencies – family, school, the media, higher and adult education, etc – is the next question. The type of compulsory schooling that a child needs is to be determined by seeing what parts of the total package of essential learnings is most appropriately carried out in schools rather than other places. All sorts of practical considerations may be expected to come into the picture here – the unlikelihood that a certain type of learning will occur in the family; the need to lay early foundations for another kind of learning rather than leaving this to post-school institutions, and so on.

Given all this, the *extent* of compulsory schooling that a child needs is still an open question. We should not assume from the outset that it should take up most of the day. In Britain we have traditionally made this assumption, but there are no solid grounds for it. As mentioned earlier, not every other country makes compulsory schooling so extensive. Britain begins it at age five; elsewhere it is often six or seven. Britain has a schoolday lasting through both morning and afternoon. Other places – not only the old Soviet Union, but contemporary Germany, among others – restrict school to a long morning session, leaving children – and teachers – more time for their own affairs.

In the twenty-first century, we should not jettison the idea that schools should mirror the larger society in their management of time. But we would do well to jettison the centrality assumption which both share. Work in both areas needs to be dispassionately reviewed to see how much and what types of it are necessary. In the adult world the global amount of work should be cut down in the interests of leaving people more time for autonomous activities of their own choice. Schools should follow suit. At this point the mirroring might seem to vanish, since children, especially younger children, are not yet autonomous agents. But they are autonomous agents in the making and doing the kinds of things that fully autonomous persons do can prepare them in their turn for autonomy. Aristotle famously wrote that 'the things we have to learn before we can do them, we learn by doing them, e.g. men become builders by building and lyre-players by playing the lyre; so too we become just by doing just acts, temperate by doing temperate acts, brave by doing brave acts.' (*Nicomachean Ethics*, II.1). We can add to this that we also become autonomous by doing autonomous acts.

Children may not yet see the whole picture of a life of autonomous well-being, but they can participate in some of the components of it. One of these is unconstrained activity; another is selection of goals from an array of options. Something like the de-ideologised and non-indoctrinatory vision of the Pioneer ideal might fit this bill. Imagine children, their compulsory stint of learning ended for the day, being able to choose activities from a wide menu, including practical, creative, sporting options as well as more academic ones. In *Towards a Compulsory Curriculum* I stated that whether children took part in this pro-gramme would be up to them; they could decline to do so if they preferred. I took this line because it seemed to follow from the libertarian starting-point I had adopted: there seemed no good reason to put any constraint on the child given that the compulsory learning period took care of overriders. But, having changed ethical allegiance and gone straight for autonomous well-being rather than for liberty, I now think there is a case for making all children take part in the option-system and not giving them the choice of dropping out (unless there are good reasons). The case rests, obviously enough, on what is needed for autonomy. Just as future lyre-players have to practise on the lyre, so future autonomes have to have practise choosing between options and weighing one preference against another. Younger children need to be deliberately inducted into this. As they get older and more like autonomous adults, there will be less need for constraint and the activities could become purely voluntary.

But does not *making* children participate in the option-system blur the dis-tinction, so clear-cut in *Towards a Compulsory Curriculum*, between the block of compulsory learning and the 'Pioneer' activities? Only partly. For there would still be a vital difference between the Science or the Personal and Social Education lessons children did in the mornings and the clay-modelling or bad-minton they did after lunch. The Science and PSE classes would be unavoidable: they would have to attend them, like it or no. But they would not have to do the clay-modelling or badminton: they might choose car-repairing or drama instead. True, they would have to do something or other in the option-system. They wouldn't have the further option of going home early. But in any case, given the psychology of younger children, they would be unlikely to *feel* a sense of con-straint: what would be likely to be phenomenologically more present to them is the freedom they have to try different things of their own choice.

I have concentrated on the option-system, but there is more to say about the compulsory classes. These would be reserved for essential learning. What this should consist in is a longer story than I can tell here, although I made something of a start on it in section 2.2 above. But I do want to make one or two points which relate to work, especially to the centrality assumption. As things are now, the long school day is taken as read in British educational planning. It is a kind of grid which has to be filled in with varied activities. A school timetable is a concrete representation of this more abstract idea. The whole period of compulsory schooling, from five to sixteen, can be seen as a larger grid, a vast concatenation of timetabled slots which must somehow be filled.

The central question, at school or national level, then becomes 'How can all this time be best used?' not 'What do children need to learn?' At national level this has been the approach to the construction of the National Curriculum. The ten foundation subjects were revealed to us out of the blue. There was no suggestion that they were derived from reflection on what it was necessary for pupils to know or do or be. They were the traditional content of the secondary school grid and the government merely imposed this grid on the primary world too. The work that the subject working groups then did in working out syllabuses in history, maths and so on was the detailed colouring-in of the general framework, bearing in mind that they were dealing with so many years of learning, so many weeks each year and so many hours in each week: what they came up with would have to be appropriate to this given structure. So would the priorities that had to be established between different subject-matters across the curriculum in their competition for timetabled space. The result of all this, as we now know, was a curriculum bursting at its seams, with too much packed into it to fit its own grid. The Dearing Report (Dearing 1994) sliced it down to size. In this, as everywhere else, the first consideration was 'How can the time available best be used?'

It is ironic that Sir Keith Joseph, the intellectual herald and foundations-digger of the National Curriculum, should have made it an early priority of his to rid the curriculum of what he called 'clutter'. His instinct was right. So much subject-matter had found its way into the curriculum whose only rationale was as a time-filler of timetabled space. The way forward should have been to start on a different basis – to ask what children really needed to learn. But as it turned out, the pre-Dearing National Curriculum became a beacon for the clutter-moth.

One of the things that drove me to write *Towards a Compulsory Curriculum* was the gut-feeling that a lot of things were being taught in compulsory classes for which no good reason seemed available. As well as swathes of factual material within subjects, history and geography not least, there were also whole subjects themselves. I could not see why there should be compulsory modern languages (and neither could my colleague at the Institute of Education who was Head of Modern Languages at the time, Alan Hornsey (1969)). Creative arts activities were also questionable, their place in the curriculum sun often being justified around that time (the late 1960s and early 1970s) by educational theories of some luxuriance. Physical education was likewise something whose place seemed securer in the 'Pioneer' system than in the compulsory curriculum. So were practical subjects like woodwork or metalwork, at that time a staple of the curriculum, at least for many 'less able' boys.

The compulsory curriculum before and after the 1988 Education Reform Act has been based on the assumption that children should be constrained to work (heteronomously) at school subjects for the major part of their time. In this it has not so much mirrored as been a leading instance of the doctrine of the centrality of work. As this doctrine wears thinner in the adult world we may hope that its erosion will be reflected in new thinking about where curriculum planning should originate. But schools need not just reflect society. If the larger changes in attitudes to work are to come about sooner rather than later, the education system can play a part, along with the media, in initiating them. Schools do not *have* to have the time-grids which have become second nature to them. Governments could change them without too much difficulty. They would then have to give more thought to what was essential to children's learning, but that would be no bad thing. Apart from that, they might even save a bit of money by reducing compulsory territory and introducing a perhaps less costly options-system.

In addition, the problem that we touched on in Chapter 1 of motivating pupils who do not want to learn what they are made to learn would surely be eased, with financial as well as psychological benefits all round, not least for bill-footing governments. I have always had sympathy with such 'problem' youngsters where their uncooperativeness derives from the obligatoriness of school structures, the inclusion of subject matter which has to be learnt for no good reason, or an often justified feeling that schools don't have their own well-being clearly at heart. If their compulsory classes were about things patently and directly about their own and others' flourishing, perhaps they would find them more appealing. And if a large part of their day were constructed around their preferred activities, the motivational problems should be even less.

In July 1995 the Department for Education was merged – significantly for the theme of this book – into a new Department for Education and Employment. In the same month its new Secretary of State, Gillian Sheppard, introduced plans to provide more work-based education for demotivated 14-year-olds. As well as helping children, she stated that it could 'do something useful for employers at the same time.' The changes, she added, would be for teenagers 'itching' to get out into the world of work. 'You would be surprised how many children see the point of turning up on time when they understand what is required of them by adults and it is not some irritant imposed on them by schools.' (*Times Educational Supplement*, 21 July 1995)

This seems to be giving early induction into the regime of work priority over education. This kind of solution to poor motivation provides new motives to work hard, but at a different sort of work from schoolwork – namely, at factory- or office-work. It is a late manifestation of the British tradition of treating work as at life's core and education as subservient to it.

This is not to say that work-experience should have no place in a remodelled school system. It might find a place within the compulsory curriculum – perhaps as part of a programme of understanding the structure of industry, or within the option system, tailored to pupil inclinations but not imposed on those who have other kinds of preference. But all this would have to be carefully thought through, tied into the overall structure of aims and values, and part of every pupil's provision. It would not be a one-shot policy tacked on to a failing structure.

A proper work-experience programme might well be helpful motivationally. But here I'm thinking about motivation as something within the educational domain, not outside it. Work-experience would have no priority vis-à-vis other forms of motivation – for why should work be taken to be of special importance?

The compulsory and the option systems together would be designed to keep up pupils' interest in learning. Practical understanding – in both its senses of [a] (mental or physical) skills and [b] the application of practical reason to the conduct of one's life – would play a larger role than traditionally and would be more attractive, conjoined with more theoretical forms of learning, than an unpalatable diet of facts to be recalled. Schoolwork would be wholly at the service of pupils' developing desire-structures as autonomous adults in the making. A motivational charge would thus be built into it from the start. Knowledge to be acquired would no longer, as in too many cases today, be detached from the child's desires, actual or in formation[3]. Schoolwork based on personally meaningless knowledge of this kind would no longer prepare pupils for a lifetime of that 'personally non-significant' adult work first referred to on p 6 above.

Pupils' motivation should also benefit from the crumbling of conventional attitudes to work which identify the mid- to late teens as the time of life when fundamental vocational decisions are made. If work is no longer life's rationale, the pressure to choose one's path ahead should diminish. (As we saw on p 45, 'life-planning' is not an irremovable part of the autonomous life). Some youngsters would still want to make these fateful commitments, but whether they do so would be up to them as autonomous persons: neither they nor anybody else would be leant on, urged or forced to do so.

For most pupils the kind of learning they experienced in school would no longer vanish for ever once their vocational orientation was fixed. There is no good reason why academic learning should be confined, as it has been for most, to the first sixteen or twenty years of life. It is only our attachment to the centrality of work that makes us think this way: academic learning stops when work begins. Dropping centrality allows learning activities to seep beyond their juvenile frontiers, to spread and fructify wherever they are wanted. In this, as in so much else, the end of work's dominion should make our lives so much less tense, perhaps even – in some quarters – of near-Californian relaxedness.

POST-SCHOOL LEARNING

In making these remarks, am I aligning myself with advocates of 'lifelong learning' or 'the learning society'? I would rather not use these terms, as they mean different things in different contexts and their employment may be more confusing than helpful. For one thing, they can be appropriated by traditionalist supporters of the work culture. These argue that in an age when few jobs will be for life, people must be prepared for frequent, often quite radical, changes of jobs and to undertake the retraining this requires. Others take a more liberal line. We need lifelong learning, not only and not primarily, for economic reasons, but also, and mainly, for personal development. While there is something to be said for both positions – and my sympathies are, unastonishingly, more with the latter – my liberal inclinations make me suspicious of any pressure, moral or otherwise, put on people to feel that they *should* keep on learning throughout their lives. Of course, all of us excluding the brain-damaged will constantly be picking up new bits of knowledge as our experience changes; but proponents of life-long learning or the learning society have more than this in view. For one thing, quotidian learning of this kind has always existed, but the call for lifelong learning has come in the light of social changes towards the end of the twentieth century. 'Learning' in this context refers to more substantial achievement: following a course, systematically teaching oneself, acquiring skills on the job.

No doubt, in a society not longer in thrall to work, but where what work there is demands more retraining, more adults will spend more time than now on recreational as well as vocational learning. But to call this a 'learning society' may mislead. I still prefer Dahrendorf's notion of the 'activity society', since this indicates the ideal that everyone should be able to engage in activities, whether productive or otherwise, of his or her own autonomous choice. Many, perhaps nearly all, of these agents will be drawn towards new forms of learning in the more substantial sense. But some may not be. They may want to do the sorts of things they have always done. In a 'learning society' where the expectation is that everyone will want to learn, our conservatives may feel pariahs. I think this would be unfortunate.

I am sure there is much more to be said about post-school learning in Scenario 2, but I have little further to say about it myself. Having covered several thousand words on parental and school education and only reached the adolescent, I half-feel that I *ought* to be able to generate four or five times as many to do justice to the rest of a human lifetime. But misplaced obligations aside, priority should rightly go to arrangements for the early years. This must be so if education, i.e. upbringing, is our target. As we saw earlier (p 80), cultural educators pursue this objective beyond childhood, but this is a residual and small-scale enterprise as compared with the education of the young.

Whilst, like the lifelong educators, I envisage (for Scenario 2) a proliferation of adult learning, I believe there is a case for *simplifying* present structures. In

Britain, for instance, Further Education is administratively separated from Higher Education, while Adult Education can lie outside both. Administrative divisions generate theoretical rationalia: witness the growth industry of Higher Education studies in recent years. This has encouraged the idea that Higher Education is a phenomenon in its own right, intellectually as well as bureaucratically to be distinguished from Further Education.

I have criticised this last contention elsewhere (White 1997). A point I did *not* make in that critique is that the divisions which we now make between areas of post-school learning are themselves products of the work-society. In Britain, one of the things separating Higher Education from Further is that the former gives access to a different range of jobs from the latter, broadly speaking professional and managerial rather than at the technician level. Adult Education, as traditionally understood, has been the province of leisure- rather than work-learning. As such it has been especially associated with older people, in this context people in their twenties and above. Further and Higher Education have been predominantly for young people between sixteen and twenty-one or so preparing themselves for a career.

As we move – *if* we move – towards Scenario 2, we may expect these divisions to become less salient. The main distinction of interest to educators should be that between compulsory and post-compulsory education. In this context, 'compulsory' education includes home upbringing as well as schooling. I have in mind here that, until they become autonomous adults, children have to be educated within a framework which others lay down for them. Getting the framework right, for both home and school, is an important and complicated task. But once young people cross the line between being subject to legitimate paternalism on the part of their mentors and becoming autonomous agents, responsible for their own lives, the kinds of learning in which they choose to engage beyond this point flow from their own preferences.

In Scenario 2 these post-school preferences will not be so subjugated to work's imperatives. Activity will be the leitmotif, not necessarily productive activity. Of course, there will still need to be myriad courses at all kinds of levels in all the kinds of areas that FE and HE have covered, as well as in recreational areas not included in these. But how they should be organised – within what kinds of structures and institutions – will still have to be worked out. There will be less and less reason to follow present fracture-lines, since these are so patently tied to the work-society. It may well be better not to have rigid divisions between spheres, with hierarchies among them reflecting, as they do now, internal hierarchies between [a] levels of the work force (as in the HE/FE dichotomy), and [b] the more important realm of work and the less important realm of leisure (as in the distinction between HE and FE on the one side and Adult Education on the other). We could imagine, instead, a *seamless range* of courses of varying lengths, levels and foci.

CONCLUSION

So much energy in the present school and post-school system is channelled not into creative directions, but into nurturing conventional patterns of work. Already conditioned to take its centrality as read, pupils' minds are increasingly turned as they grow older to where they personally will end up on the great Snakes and Ladders board ahead of them. They are urged and goaded to equip themselves for one of the 'better' jobs we discussed in Chapter 1, driving themselves and their teachers through immense labours for a clutch of certificates and a ticket to success. Under any reformed system, competition will still exist for 'better' jobs and this is bound to be reflected in educational arrangements. There are no utopian solutions. But I hope the argument of this book has at least indicated the direction in which we might now go. The centrality assumption is not, in any case, as solid a part of our social life as it once was. It ought to be possible, gradually, to reduce its sway. As this happens, and as people have more of their lives for their own autonomous concerns, the wasteful scramble for 'better' jobs will come to seem that bit more pointless. With its diminution, pressures on schools and colleges to prepare their charges for it can also be expected to grow less. The year 2000 may not bring in the millennium in other than a chronological sense. But it may help us, over time, to get Larkin's toad more off our back.

NOTES

1. From a survey by the School Teachers' Review Body reported in *The Times Educational Supplement*, 9 August 1996. In more detail, it showed that 'primary heads work 55.7 hours a week, their deputies 54.5 hours a week and classroom teachers 50.8 hours. Secondary heads work 61.7 hours, deputies 56.5, department heads 53 and classroom teachers 50.3. However one in ten primary heads is working up to 70 hours a week as is one in five secondary heads.'
2. I am indebted to my colleagues Richard Aldrich and David Crook for drawing this DfEE material to my attention.
3. See White (1990) pp 120–121, 127–128 on the related notion of 'unattached instrumental knowledge'.

Bibliography

Anthony, P. D. (1977) *The Ideology of Work* London: Tavistock

Arendt, H. (1958) *The Human Condition* New York: Doubleday Anchor

Aristotle *Nicomachean Ethics*

Arneson, R. J. (1987) 'Meaningful Work and Market Socialism' *Ethics* Vol 97

Attfield, R. (1984) 'Work and the Human Essence' *Journal of Applied Philosophy* Vol 1 No 1

Central Statistical Office (1989) *Social Trends 19* London: HMSO (1995) *Social Trends 25* London: HMSO

Chang, J. (1993) *Wild Swans* London: Flamingo

Clarke, F. (1923) *Essays in the Politics of Education* Oxford: Oxford University Press

Dahrendorf, R. (1982) *On Britain* London: British Broadcasting Corporation

Dearing, R. (1994) *The National Curriculum and its Assessment: Final Report* London: School Curriculum and Assessment Authority

Dewey, J. (1915) *The School and Society* Chicago: University of Chicago Press

DfEE (1995a) Press notice 210/95
    (1995b) *The English Education System: an overview of structure and policy*

Doyal L. and Gough I. (1991) *A Theory of Human Need* London: Macmillan

Elster, J. (1985) *Making Sense of Marx* Cambridge: Cambridge University Press

Giddens, A. (1995) *Beyond Left and Right* Cambridge: Polity Press

Gough, I. (1996) 'Justifying Basic Income? A Review of Philippe van Parijs, *Real Freedom for All*' *Imprints* Vol 1 No 1

Gorz, A. (1985) *Paths to Paradise: on the Liberation from Work* London: Pluto Press

Grint, K. (1991)*The Sociology of Work: an Introduction* Cambridge: Polity Press

Heidegger, M. (1962) *Being and Time* Oxford: Basil Blackwell

Herbst, P. (1973) 'Work, Labour and University Education' in R S Peters (ed) *The Philosophy of Education* Oxford: Oxford University Press

Hornsey, A. (1969) 'Why teach a foreign language?' *Institute of Education University of London Bulletin*, No 18

Hutton, W. (1995) *The State We're In* London: Jonathan Cape

Marx, K. and Engels, F. (1965) *The German Ideology* London: Lawrence and Wishart

Moore, G. E. (1903) *Principia Ethica* Cambridge: Cambridge University Press

Nietzsche, F. (1974) *The Gay Science* New York: Vintage Books

Norman, R. (1983) *The Moral Philosophers* Oxford: Clarendon Press

O'Hear, P. and White, J. (1991) *A National Curriculum for All* London: IPPR

Pahl, R.E. (ed) (1988) *On Work: Historical, Comparative and Theoretical Approaches* Oxford: Blackwell

Paxman, J. (1991) *Friends in High Places* London: Penguin Books

Pring, R (1995) *Closing the Gap* London: Hodder and Stoughton

Rawls, J. (1971) *A Theory of Justice* Cambridge: Harvard University Press

Rifkin, J (1995) *The End of Work* New York: Tarcher/Putman

Russell, B. (1960) *In Praise of Idleness* London: Unwin Books

Rybczynski, S. A. W. (1991) *Waiting for the Weekend* New York: Viking

Sayers, S. (1988) 'The Need to Work: a Perspective from Philosophy' in Pahl, R. E. (ed) (1988)

Schwartz, A. (1982) 'Meaningful Work' *Ethics* Vol 92

Skillen, A. (1996) 'Can virtue be taught – especially these days?' *Papers of Philosophy of Education Society of Great Britain Annual Conference*

Slote, M. (1989) *Beyond Optimising* Cambridge, Mass: Harvard University Press

Tawney, R. H. (1926) *Religion and the Rise of Capitalism* West Drayton: Penguins (1966) *The Radical Tradition* Harmondsworth: Penguin Books

Taylor, C. (1989) *Sources of the Self* Cambridge: Cambridge University Press

Telfer, E. (1987) 'Leisure' in Evans, J D (ed) *Moral Philosophy and Contemporary Problems* Cambridge: Cambridge University Press

Toynbee, P. (1995) 'Whatever happened to nine to five?' *The Independent* (Magazine Section) June 10

van Parijs, P. (1995) *Real Freedom for All* Oxford: Clarendon Press

Walzer, M. (1983) *Spheres of Justice* Oxford: Martin Robertson

Warnock, M. (1977) *Schools of Thought* London: Faber and Faber

Weil, S. (1977) 'Factory Work' in Panichas, G. (ed) *Simone Weil Reader* New York: Moyer Bell

White, J. (1973) *Towards a Compulsory Curriculum* London: Routledge and Kegan Paul
(1990) *Education and the Good Life* London: Kogan Page
(1994a) 'Education and Recognition' *Paedeusis* Vol 7 No 2
(1994b) ' The Dishwasher's Child: education and the end of egalitarianism' *Journal of Philosophy of Education* Vol 28 no 2
(1995) *Education and personal well-being in a secular universe* London: Institute of Education University of London
(1997) 'Philosophy and the aims of higher education' *Studies in Higher Education* Vol 22 No 1
Williams, B. (1981) *Moral Luck* Cambridge Cambridge University Press
(1985) *Ethics and the Limits of Philosophy* London: Fontana

Index

activity 4, 7, 10, 102–3 and *passim*
 – non-work types of 4, 21, 26, 46, 52–3, 102–3
activity society, the 63, 118
Anthony, P. 13, 37
Arendt, H. 12, 36–9, 40
Aristotle 12, 63, 88, 89, 92, 114
Arneson, R. 33–5
Attfield, R. 23–5

Beck, B. 21
Berlin, I. 53
Britain 11, 12–15, 19, 42–4, 56, 59, 70, 74–5, 104–7, 115–6

career (*see also* life-planning, vocation) 94
Clarke, F. 17
consumers 9, 58, 74
cultural educators 80–1, 84–5, 118
curriculum 72, 104–111, 115
 – control 73

Dahrendorf, R. 2, 7, 8, 15–16, 56, 59, 60, 63–5, 118
Dearden, R. 59
Department for Education and Employment (DfEE) 105, 116
Dewey, J. 97
Doyal, L. 25, 51

ecology 59–60
education 16–18, chs 4, 5
 – adult 84, 119
 – aims of 3, 71, 81–96, 107–8
   – knowledge/understanding aims 85–6, 91, 108
   – skill aims 108
   – moral aims 86–90
   – personal aims 89–92
   – work aims 71–2, 92–6
 – compulsory/voluntary 111–7
 – family 82–3, 101–4
 – further 119
 – higher 36–7, 83, 119
 – post-school 118–9
 – school 16–18, 71–3, 104–117

 – school day 111–7
 – as upbringing 57, 81–5
 – vocational 71–2
 – work-experience in 116–7
equality 66
Elster, J. 21–2

flourishing life (*see* personal well-being)
full employment 12, 24–5, 43

gender 76–7, 95–6
Giddens, A. 19, 95
Gorz, A. 30, 61–3, 65
Gough, I. 25, 41, 51
Grint, K. 3, 4, 7

Heidegger, M. 38
Herbst, P. 36–7
Hornsey, A. 115
human essence 21, 23–5
Hutton, W. 11, 65, 70

job-enlargement 33

Kant, I. 88

Labour Party 12–13, 43
Larkin, P. 1, 120
learning and work, concepts of 97–101
learning society, the 118
leisure 7, 11–12, 62–3
life-planning 44, 45–6, 94–5, 117

major goals 45–6, 49–53, 57 and *passim*
Marx, K. 12–13, 21–3, 24, 27, 28, 29, 52
Marxism 2, 6, 12, 28–9
Moore, G. 52–3
morality 86–90
 – moral obligation 17, 42, 60

National Curriculum 16, 18, 73, 82, 105–111, 115
need
 – basic needs 47–8, 49
 – need for autonomous work 51–3
 – work as a basic need 3, 21–3, 25–9, 47

Nietzsche, F. 40–41, 76, 88
Norman, R. 20, 26–8, 40, 51–2

O'Hear, P. 107, 108

paid employment 3, 10, 28
 – 'good' jobs 14–15, 17, 18, 50
parents 82–3, 101–4
Patten, J. 69
personal qualities (see virtues)
personal well-being 5, 22, 26, 45–8, 89–90 and
 passim
 – autonomous 25, 29, 32–6, 45–6, 48–53, 62,
 75, 90–2 and passim
Peters, R. 84
Plato 22
post-productivist world 19, chs 4, 5

Rawls, J. 45, 94
recognition 14, 46, 51, 55, 58
religion 17, 20, 32, 42, 43
 – Puritanism 8, 13, 44
Rifkin, J. 74, 75
right to work 24, 30–6
Russell, B. 2, 40, 41, 42, 59
Rybczynski, S. 11

satisficing 60
Sayers, S. 20, 28–9, 40, 51, 61–2
Schwartz, A. 32–6, 51–2
Skillen, A. 97
Slote, M. 60
Socrates 22

Taylor, C. 13–14
Tawney, R. 13
teachers and work 72–4, 104–5, 109
teaching, concept of 99–100
Telfer, E. 63
temperance 58, 104

Thrasymachus 22
Toynbee, P. 11, 15, 59

unemployment 43, 70, 71
 – education for 71
utilitarianism 59–60

van Parijs, P. 3, 41, 66–67
virtues 40–1, 57–8, 86–8, 96, 103–4
vocation 44

Walzer, M. 67
Warnock, M. 2, 25
Weil, S. 30–32, 40
Williams, B. 42, 60, 95
work
 – autonomous 3, 5, 7, 35–6, 48–53 and passim
 – autonomous agency in 7, 10, 35–6, 51, 53,
 68 n.1
 – centrality of 2, 10–14, 16, 19, 27–8, 35, 38,
 39, 40–44, 53, 59–64, 69–71
 – concept of 3–10, 28
 – distribution 65–8
 – heteronomous 3, 6, 8–10, 53–60, 61–2 and
 passim
 – human nature and 20–29
 – managerial 3, 33, 35, 51, 55–6
 – meaningful 20, 23–5, 26, 30–36, 51–2
 – mechanical 30–36
 – part-time 43, 70
 – personally (non-) significant 6, 10, 14, 117
 – reduction 27, 29, 30–31, 34–5, 54–60, 61,
 74–8, 109
 – schoolwork 8, 16–18, 97–8, 107
 – (un-)willing 6, 14
 – voluntary 75
 – women's 3, 7, 76–7, 95–6
work culture, the 10–18 and passim

Young Pioneers 112